Library of
Davidson College

Micros: a pervasive force

MICROS: a pervasive force

A study of the impact of microelectronics on business and society 1946-90

Michael Orme

ASSOCIATED BUSINESS PRESS
LONDON

All Rights Reserved. No part of this publication may be reproduced, stored in a retrieval system or transmitted in any form or by any means: electronic, electrostatic, magnetic tape, mechanical, photocopying, recording or otherwise, without permission in writing from the publishers.

Published by Associated Business Press
An imprint of Associated Business Programmes Limited
Ludgate House
107-111 Fleet Street
London EC4A 2AB

First published 1979

© copyright Michael Orme 1979

ISBN 0 85227 231 6

Typeset by Photo-Graphics, Honiton, Devon
Printed and bound in Great Britain by
Redwood Burn Ltd., Trowbridge & Esher

Contents

	ACKNOWLEDGEMENTS	x
	INTRODUCTION	xii
1	THE ECONOMIC BACKGROUND TO ELECTRONICS:	1
	Industrial arthritis in the West	
	Japan's technology policy	
	Pacing microelectronics	
	The Russian lag	
	Blurred distinctions	
	Consumers are changing too	
	New consumer categories	
	The case of the home computer	
	Cheapest is best	
	Car consumption	
	Japanese consumers shape the future	
	Conclusions	

| 2 | THE SOCIAL AND POLITICAL ENVIRONMENT: | 26 |

    The future is here
    The 'job-killers'
    The future is a 'black box'
    How fast a diffusion rate?
    Transitional unemployment
    Further uncertainties: the case of AT&T
    Contending views
    The hidden key: computer simulation
    The status of information
    The second industrial revolution
    The postindustrial society: corporate structures
    Political problems
    Information is power
    Conclusions
    Appendix 2.1: The information explosion
    Appendix 2.2: Kondratief, Keynes and Electronics

| 3 | A CERTAIN SMALL DEVICE: THE HISTORICAL PERSPECTIVE | 57 |

    The engineering continuum
    Four traditions
    Making it usable

| 4 | THE MICROPROCESSOR: SCOPE AND PROSPECTS | 68 |

    Computer engineering
    Microprocessor engineering
    Threats/opportunities
    The case of autos and the middle ground

The gospel of Noyce
Forecasting flaws

5   A COMPUTER REVOLUTION:
    THE COMPUTER AS A COMPONENT   81
    A computer revolution
    Everything merges and disperses
    Information-processing pathologies
    A touch of 'lock-in'
    IBM moves
    Its all database
    Distributed DP in sum
    Telematics
    The impact of gadget computing
    Conclusions

6   THE HUMAN ENGINEERING PROBLEM:
    LIMITS ON THE FUTURE   98
    The digital timepiece vibrates the future
    Not just myopia
    Managers must change too
    Where are the design engineers?
    Consultants flourish
    Programming problems
    Too few programmers
    Not just electronics
    Conclusions
    Appendix 6.1: Micro talk

7   SEMICONDUCTORS: THE WORLD'S
    TOUGHEST BUSINESS   120
    Force-feeding the market

Making the products usable
A unique industry
Quoting below costs
A little history
Shifting from science to technology
The force of the learning curve
Japan Inc. runs it hard
Why Europe lags
Korea bids for customers and supremacy
Fairchild microcosm of an industry
Designer interaction
The strange case of Inmos
The Barron philosophy
Parameter companies
Conclusions

8 SILICON FUTURES 147

The general characteristics of silicon products
The marketing history of the calculator
The calculator Mark II
Lots of computers in the home
The 'intelligent' phone
Locked into the home
Who wants sophisticated electronics?
Programs or dedication?
The age of the utility
More personal gadgets
The automobile
Transforming the car engine
The GM check list

The auto industry 'learning curve'
Appendix 8.I: The reinvention of the telephone and the TV receiver

9   **NETWORKS TO THE FUTURE**   173

A $400 billion information industry
Computer networks *vs* roads
What about the price of oil?
A huge economic battle
The age of the satellite
Japan's glass fibre city
Heartland America
IBM's systems network architecture
Europe may lag
The AT&T case study
Conclusions
Appendix 9.1: Electronic mail
Appendix 9.2: Satellites: business uses space technology

EPILOGUE: COMPUTERS BREAK LOOSE:
The Emergence of the UIM   191

GLOSSARY   197

BIBLIOGRAPHY AND REFERENCES   205

INDEX   209

Acknowledgements

This book could not have been written without the immense patience and grasp of the subject matter of a large number of people in and around the electronics industry, who were prepared to give me much of their time and take pains to answer my questions intelligibly. I would like to acknowledge in particular the following, although many others have been involved too:
Howard Losty of GEC, Si Lyle of Digital Equipment, Jerry Wasserman of Arthur D. Little, Jeff Samson of STC, Dr Ian Mackintosh of Mackingtosh Consultants, Tom Lawrence of Intel, Iann Barron of Inmos, Mal Northrop of Rockwell and Glen Madland of Integrated Circuit Engineering.

Needless to say any errors of judgement, interpretation or fact are entirely the author's responsibility. I also thank Ron Condon, the Editor of Datalink, for commissioning a series of articles in 1976 which first made me focus my interest in the engineering industry onto microelectronics. I am most grateful, as well, to my publishers, my editor and production editor, for turning the manuscript into a book so quickly. This means that hostages to fortune in a notoriously fast-changing area will have been kept to a minimum.

I am deeply grateful to my wife Giuliana, who not only typed much of the manuscript but also put up with my sometimes saturnine mood. I want, finally, to express my gratitude to the late Professor C.D. Broad, for teaching me that 'the factors which we were aware of or can take account of are always a meagre selection from those which are in fact relevant and effective; the remote consequences even of that meagre selection can seldom be predicted with any accuracy.'

Introduction

"All prediction is difficult, especially about the future."

Nils Bohr

Anyone studying the background to microelectronics does well to remember Montaigne's sage comment: 'I believe everything I hear down to the smallest detail, but with reservations.' This strikes just the right note between a refusal to be surprised and underlying scepticism. This is an admirable double standard, if that is what it is, to apply when analysing the claims and counter claims of electronics experts in particular. In microelectronics, claims which seen absurd often turn out to be true; but at the same time, technical virtuosity often (almost always) underrates the difficulty in applying these innovations, and the snags presented by what has been called 'the human engineering problem'.

It is now well known, following a justly commended special issue of the *Scientific American* in September 1977 and a spate of popular articles in mass-circulation newspapers and magazines, that a technology is now in place (and has been for nearly a decade) to transform almost every sector of industry and commerce and almost every social institution. The main qualities of that technology — semiconductor technology — are as follows:

- It makes possible the widespread substitution of an algorithm ('decision rule' or program encoded in a computer) for human judgement — at least at a low level. It therefore extends or even displaces human brainpower.
- It is so compact in its physical embodiment that virtually no field of manufacturing, the utilities, the service industries or commerce is left untouched — in many cases in a fundamental way in terms of organisation and/or product visualisation.
- Not only is it incredibly cheap, but progressively so. Since the early 1960s, during a period of historically high inflation and generally rising industrial costs, the price of each unit of electronic performance has fallen one hundred thousandfold.
- The speed of advance has been without parallel in the development of a major technology. The performance of a single integrated circuit, measured by the number of 'logic-gates' it can contain, has increased ten thousandfold in fifteen years.
- Already the reliability of semiconductor devices far exceeds that of any other engineering device to date, and continues to improve. This means that such devices, despite replacement costs, become increasingly attractive compared with mechanical and electromechanical components — viz., cash registers and telephone exchanges.
- Because at present levels of complexity microprocessors are programmable (or, as 'dedicated' systems, easily and cheaply replaceable) their performance can be adjusted. This has not happened with earlier engineering controls.

All this results from the exploitation and mass-production, over the past decade, of increasingly densely-packed and cheap integrated circuit components. In practice this has mainly involved silicon-based integrated circuits (SICs), better known as 'silicon chips'. This electronic technology, concerned with the processing, storage and amplification of signals, data and information, promises to transform the business scene during the 1980s, as well as the societies within which industry and commerce operate whether they be capacious, continental economies like the USA, mixed economies like those of Britain and Scandinavia, big business dominated, but tightly-planned economies such as Japan and South Korea, or centrally-planned, resource-concentrated systems like China and the USSR. Much less clear is how, when, how quickly and how deeply this transformation will actually occur.

Even without the emergence of a new 'heartland' technology, which advanced electronics is poised to become, the world has been a progressively less predictable place during the 1970s. This has been due to a complex of factors. Main amongst them, on the economic front,. have been the fast growth in manufacturing capacity in 'low wage zones', the growth in 'discretionary' incomes and personal savings in the West, together with the steady erosion of the 'producer ethic' (with its values based on diligence and discipline) as mass-consumer societies have appeared — although this has not been a clear-cut universal phenomenon: viz., Japan and West Germany.

One result of these changes has been the difficulty in plotting the likely behaviour of consumers, both in terms of total demand and the pattern of demand. Governments, for instance, have found that tax increases have sometimes been accompanied by rises in personal spending and vice versa, and businesses have found that just when they expect consumers to spend more on their products, people increase their savings and shift their pattern of demand. A notable example of the consumer 'black box' occurred with the pocket calculator (perhaps the best example, so far, of the pervasive power of microelectronics). Quite simply no one knew whether people would want pocket calculators until they actually became available. The calculator may have been an 'electronic' slide-rule but its charisma was far brighter and spread far wider than that of the product it has replaced. Significantly, the semiconductor majors were surprised by the success of the small assembly companies selling the first electronic calculators to whom they supplied the components. They themselves then moved into the market: but not until the small entrepreneurs had led the way. But even then, by 1977, despite huge sales of calculators, many of the producers showed 'red ink' because the market became so competitive and the price-cutting was so fierce. In short, it was a rerun of the semiconductor market itself.

Most forecasting methods that make any pretence at being 'scientific' are based on prediction: this is, an extrapolation of existing trends. The cultural changes cited above have cast doubts on the feasibility of such forecasting. These doubts become, by definition, even more severe when it is recognised that basic technological parameters are on the point of changing with microelectronics moving into a more pervasive phase. This presents a major discontinuity, which makes linear forecasting an almost certainly futile exercise — unless it is what is known as 'normative' forecasting such as occurred with the NASA-Apollo project and is now in process with the drive in Japanese industry to develop and use microelectronics as an essential ingredient in Japan's export strategy for the 1980s.

Apart from 'normative' forecasting, the postwar world is littered with examples (some of which are set out in Chapter 2) of the inability of experts and business executives to forecast the shape of the future in their own specialisms and sectors, let alone other people's. This is why we reject in this book the intellectual fad of the 1970s, the 'Think Tank' and the Delphi method it has spawned. At the Rand Corporation, one of the first to enter this lucrative field, they talk about 'opinion technology' via the Delphi process. This is based on the premise that X heads are better than one in making a forecast. The Delphi method involves asking a number of experts to make a prediction. The first estimates are then tallied and the resulting opinions fed back to the experts, who then reflect on the first-round thoughts of the other experts. Eventually some sort of consensus emerges. But despite the fact that the Delphi method looks somehow 'scientific', it is no more likely to be reliable than any other method, given some of the underlying comments made above.

Naturally, the author has spoken to a large number of experts in the process of compiling this book, but has tended to contrast their views rather than try to lump them into some sort of consensus. The basic point remains: however scientific in their methods futurologists and forecasters may appear to be, most business and government policy has to be based on what is not known rather than what is known.

Tacit assumptions have had to be made in this book, which may turn out to be very wrong, about the likely course of the component technology. One of the main such assumptions is that silicon technology is here to stay through much of the 1980s and that the thrust of the semiconductor industry will remain technological rather than basically scientific. But even if that is a correct assumption, the commercial development of such technologies as Josephson junctions and electron beam circuit tracing may have an impact on semiconductor devices more quickly and more dramatically than has often been allowed. But on the other hand, while the semiconductor industry is organised to supply mass-market requirements, it may be found that less complex and more readily usable circuits, rather than very advanced ones, are called for.

What is not in doubt is that the most reliable and compact control devices are now available, which can control the simplest systems in a cost-effective way or add electronic intelligence to products which had not previously incorporated even primitive algorithms. Nevertheless, as we see in Chapter 5, there are still considerable practical obstacles in the way of designing such components into devices: obstacles which will make the going very tough for a lot of businesses in the 1980s.

Following a chapter on the broad economic background to the world electronics industry, the next three chapters set out to place electronic devices in the engineering continuum; explain what a microprocessor is and also the error in using the term microprocessor to cover all microelectronic components; and then show that the development of highly complex electronic circuits is in essence a computer revolution. The basic point to emerge is that considerable computing power need no longer be associated, necessarily, with a large and costly piece of equipment, built up from thousands of components, but can itself be a simple and very cheap component. This has very wide implications. It makes the computer an unimportant piece of equipment in the total machine and equipment environment in terms of cost and availability. It also means that computing power can be distributed virtually wherever it is needed, because the distinction is becoming progressively blurred between mainframe, mini and microcomputers, as well as between these computers and such pieces of equipment as typewriters, copying machines and input/output terminals. At the same time, there is a growing tendency, due to electronic componentry, for digital computers and data-transmission networks to share the same basic semiconductor components. This is the basis of the real 'computer-information' revolution. The technological merger is described in Chapter 4 and the possible and astonishing repercussions of computer networks are set out in some detail in Chapter 9. In addition, some of the broad social and corporate issues involved in computer networking are implicit in many of views put forward in Chapter 2.

In a sense, the key chapters are 5 and 6, which analyse some of the short-term forces which will determine the pace at which semiconductor technology is actually diffused, as well as some of the practical difficulties facing the business community at large over the next decade. The main forces thus considered, although not necessarily in order of treatment, are as follows:

- the actual and potential supply of design engineers capable of working with 'electronic intelligence' rather than with mechanical and/or electromechanical components. There will almost certainly be a serious shortage of such engineers.
- The general resistance of business managements to production processes and office procedures very different from the traditional systems and the growing need to visualise products and services which incorporate electronic intelligence.
- The world's software capability: whether it is growing fast enough, irrespective of the supply of design engineers capable of working with electronic components, to keep the current world population of computers busy, let alone pursue potential applications.
- The ability of either the semiconductor manufacturers and/or

the end-users to make electronic circuits easier to connect and easier to program.
- The need for a probably already oversupplied semiconductor industry, which tends towards 'vertical' rather than 'horizontal' integration, to force-feed suppliers of mass-markets with circuits.
- The pace at which Japanese industry successfully incorporates advanced circuitry into its offices, factories and into its end-products for the world market, which could force the pace for much of US and European industry and commerce.

Chapter 8 analyses the main markets for circuits and studies case histories of certain silicon products. There is a final chapter which looks at the possible repercussions arising from the fifth and sixth generation of computers based on incredibly complex circuits, which seems to be a suitable epilogue.

The author's conclusion, after a long and intellectually taxing journey through the field, is that it will only be when the children at present being brought up with calculators and computers achieve (it is to be hoped) a better symbiosis than our generation has managed with computers, and become the design engineers of the 1990s, that the shape of the electronic future will be clearer. Meanwhile, what will almost certainly be an uncomfortable transition period is starting. As one electronics executive has put it 'the silicon chip is like a key, that without warning, has unlocked a door against which many products and technologies have been pressing. The door has suddenly flown open and those industries (and engineers) who are unprepared may find themselves in a heap on the other side.'

1 The economics background to the electronics industry

> "if animal spirits are dimmed and the spontaneous optimism falters, leaving us to depend on nothing but mathematical expectation, enterprise will fade and die; — though fears of loss may have a basis no more reasonable than hopes of profit had before."
>
> *John Maynard Keynes*

The 1980s loom as a bloody battlefield for US and West European industry. This is due to three main forces in the world economy, which tend, more and more, to feed on each other.

The first is the sharp growth in productive capacity outside the industrialised world and the accelerating technology transfer, through 'turnkey' contracts and licensing agreements, between the industrialised countries and the 'surplus' population zones like China, India and Latin America. The second is the 'mature' look of a lot of traditional industries in the industrialised countries: such industries as steel, shipbuilding and, as time goes on, autos. This broadening trend towards overcapacity in the industrialised world is exacerbated, and perhaps partly caused by, the inability of governments to counter inflationary pressures (that is, rises in prices in general) or react to sharp increases in specific commodity prices (such as oil) without slowing down growth. In other words, the major failure of Keynesian economics has been that the inversion of Say's Law has not held: supply may not create its own demand but neither does demand, automatically, create its own supply. This slow growth rate (low that is, in comparison with the growth rates seen in the 1950s and 1960s, but still adequate in comparison with the average growth rate (over the past 100 years), when superimposed on the normal trade cycle, affects the amplitude of the cycle: exaggerates the 'highs' and the 'lows' and shortens the time span between them. The third major factor, which is the subject of this book, is the dramatic development of 'highstream' electronic technology, which is fast leading to the computer-information revolution, based on powerful yet incredibly cheap (in hardware terms) microminiaturised integrated circuits.

The changing industrial scene across the world is graphically illustrated by the following phenomenon. In 1978 the world steel industry emerged from the disastrous slump of 1975-7 to exceed in output terms the 1974 record of 704 million tonnes of crude steel. But steel industries in the richest countries, especially in Western Europe, remained chronically oversupplied. Back in 1973, the OECD countries (plus South Africa) accounted for two-thirds of world steel output. In 1978, the proportion had slumped to under 60 per cent. The biggest gainers have been the Eastern bloc countries, whose steel production has gone up from 30 per cent to 35 per cent of the world total during the period, and the less developed countries (the LDCs) whose share in steel production has risen from 4 per cent to 6 per cent. Moreover, the LDCs have raised their output every year since 1973.

Industrial arthritis in the West

According to top economists at GATT in Geneva, Jan Tumlir and Richard Blackhurst, the changing shape of world steel production reflects the changing shape of the world economy in general.[1] The GATT economists argue that the slowdown in the growth of the industrialised economies since 1974 may only have been exacerbated by the OPEC oil price hike of 1973, and not caused by it. The Tumlir/Blackhurst thesis, which is shared by a lot of businessmen who operate transnational companies, or who engage in direct exporting, is that a kind of 'industrial arthritis' has stiffened up much of industry in the USA and Western Europe, since the period of postwar reconstruction was completed in the 1960s, and the shift in Europe from the countryside into industry was completed.

The gradual decline of manufacturing in the West is easy to document. After growing at a compound annual rate of around 6.5 per cent in the early 1960s, overall manufacturing production in the OECD countries slipped to a rate of just over 4.5 per cent between 1970-3, and since then has been practically flat. Moreover in such sectors as steel, textiles and light manufacturing, production has actually declined in the developed countries. Theoretically, these declines should have released manpower in these countries to seek jobs in higher-technology industries, but due to policies of tariffs and outright subsidies this has not happened on the whole.

But all the while, the developed countries' traditional markets for simpler types of manufactured goods have been grabbed by the developing countries. Since the mid-1970s, while output in the developed world has been virtually stagnant, the advanced developing and less developed countries, outside the Soviet bloc, have been expanding their industrial output by 6-8 per cent a year. Thus, the developing nations' share of world trade in manufactured goods is rising. Indeed Professor Assar Lindbeck of Stockholm's Institute for International Economic Studies, predicts that by the end of this century Third World manufacturers may be handling 20 per cent of the world's industrial output compared to 7 per cent today. In fact this may understate the trend, if, as seems unlikely, China's implied current $350 billion capital investment scheme does turn China into a modern industrial economy by the 1990s, and if surplus population zones like India, Brazil and Argentina do shift their emphasis from agriculture to industry, while North America, Western Europe and Australasia provide more and more of the world's food.

All this is forcing marked changes on the industrial nations, despite the economic and political rigidities which have prevented most of them from adjusting their industries on the scale necessary for sustained growth. A notable exception has been Japan, which shows every sign of adapting quickly and dramatically to the changing face of world competition, by 'bootstrapping' itself into the new electronic and microprocessing industries. Most corporate planners in the field reckon that the industrial countries probably have a ten-year run before the Third World — or at least the more sophisticated parts of it like Korea and Brazil — start seriously to incorporate the new electronics into their products and production processes. Several Third World countries, such as Korea and Taiwan, have already started their own semiconductor industries.

Just as Japan has been eating into US and European markets in such items as colour TVs, 1-2 litre, 4-cylinder cars and popular metric ball bearing, she herself is getting pushed out of important markets by the newly industrialised countries. According to UNCTAD statistics, these countries (mainly in this case, Hongkong, Singapore, South Korea and Taiwan) have increased their share of imports into Japan from 13 per cent in 1970 to nearly 40 per cent today. At the same time, the Japanese have found themselves outgunned by these countries in important Third World markets in shipbuilding, contract work and construction and textbook cases of industry prone to takeover by newcomers — that is, those using a stable technology to produce standardised products into well-established markets. Items like radios and, more recently, TV receivers, watches and clocks and other household appliances.

Without a major change in industrial strategy, Japan feels that she will no longer be the pacesetter, but will relinquish her position to South Korea, Taiwan (and who knows, by the year 2000, China). In 1977, for example, Japan built 8.5 million cars. But now Toyota, admittedly well known for its conservative pronouncements, believes that the world car market will expand by only 35 per cent over the next decade. At the same time, should motor industries in Korea, Brazil and Argentina be developed at a faster clip, the auto industry could be facing severe overcapacity in the 1980s. With these kinds of considerations in mind, Toyota is reducing capacity to 70 per cent. At the same time, the Japanese shipbuilding industry is being ruthlessly adapted to world market conditions with shipbuilding capacity being slashed by half.

There is now a danger of serious slowdown in Japan's economic growth. All Japan's boom industries of yesteryear — cars, ships, consumer electronics (except video, calculators and watches) — face mere replacement demand at home. In export markets, Japanese industry faces rising competition from other Far Eastern producers, together with pressures from within those markets themselves. Western Europe, for instance, has excess capacity in most of these industries too. The pressure on the Japanese to keep up their export momentum are intense. Japan already has nearly the highest urban living costs in the world and by 1978 — partly reflecting the strength of the yen against the US dollar — Japanese labour costs in dollar terms were almost as high as the USA's. Moreover, the Japanese economy is based on two main but fragile pillars. First, there is the system of 'lifetime employment', which until now has meant what it said, even though it has never been put in writing from one business to another, and is simply tacitly understood. Clearly, the system is now under considerable strain. The other pillar is the updated *zaibatsu* — the linkup between business corporations, banks and government planning and devlopment agencies. Japanese corporations tend to be massively geared, far in excess of their disposable assets. This economic and financial structure and the fact that Japan, like the rest of the industrialised world, is being driven upmarket by the newly industrialising countries (a process which could well go on until India and China have got to where Korean and Taiwan are today in terms of labour costs) lies behind large-scale and methodical moves in Japan to re-rig Japanese industry; and to do so on the basis of the what will be the 'heartland' technology of the 1980s, microelectronics.

Japan's technology policy

It has long been apparent that Japan, having raced fastest to the latest stage of the world manufacturing revolution, would be one of the first to get into the post-manufacturing (or more precisely the post-industrial) revolution after that. The major difference between Japan and the rest of the industrialised world, especially the USA (which tends to run on the wastage its continental-sized economy can absorb), is that the Japanese have a technological policy. What impresses US and European observers of the Japanese scene, who talk to Japanese people from MITI — the Japanese Ministry of International Trade and Industry — is not the advanced level of Japanese research, but the fact that this research is part of a larger plan.

The industrial race over the next decade will be won by those businesses and industrial zones which can raise their productivity fastest. This will be largely determined by who can apply the new electronics most widely to information gathering, industrial controls and into end-products for the marketplace. One of the most notable analyses on this topic appeared in May 1978 in France, in the government report, *L'Informatisation de la Societe,* commissioned in 1976 by President Giscard d'Estaing, and mainly written by M. Simon Nora, a senior adviser in the French Finance Ministry. The report, which highlights much of thinking which the Japanese must have done but have kept to themselves, argues that the only way of solving the problems arising from the 'information revolution', which in turn is based on developments in microelectronics, is to create a new economic structure itself based on a clear recognition of internationally competitive and non-competitive parts of a national economy. For Nora, the crucial factor is the combination of distributed computing power with telecommunications, satellite technology and broadcasting. These together, argues the report, are going to bring about such important gains in productivity that the internationally competitive parts of the economy will diminish in social importance. This will leave a three-pronged economy. On the one hand, dying megaliths — the high employment manufacturing industries — and on the other, a mass of socially orientated organisations concerned more with providing employment than with making profits or with competing in the world marketplace. In the middle, as the dynamic part of the economy, will be a cauldron of smaller, highly computerised, innovative enterprises, on which competitiveness in the international market will depend.

But what the French have so brilliantly analysed on paper, the Japanese have long been planning and translating into practical applications. It is illustrative that Japan has been investing billions of yen in developing robots and has started to drive for self-sufficiency in advanced integrated circuit electronics in 1975. Over the past three years, it is estimated that the Japanese government will have put up at least $150 million out of a total budget of $360 million, spread between the big five in Japanese electronics (Fujitsu, Hitachi and Mitsubishi in one group and NEC and Toshiba in the other), to develop advanced versions of the silicon chip — the basic electronic component in computer and information systems. At the same time, the Japanese government has been lavishly supporting the computer industry. Although Japan has sold a few large computer systems to the USA, Australia, Spain, Korea, China and Iraq, the main emphasis seems to be on peripherals like printers, disc and tape drives and specialised computer terminals. Also latching onto the brilliant idea of Gene Amadhal, Japanese companies like Hitachi and Fujitsu have been selling copies (so-called 'plug-compatibles') of IBM machines which run on IBM software into the USA.

It is by no means clear yet where exactly the Japanese onslaught is going to be concentrated. Few experts reckon that the Japanese will seriously threaten US (and particularly IBM) control of the market in large host computers with a complex control program. More indicative, probably, is the fact that Japanese companies have seized almost 50 per cent of the US market for inexpensive electronic cash registers, which are essentially very simple computers. It is in these types of products, and in data-processing (DP) gear, where Japan is likely to look for markets to replace what cameras were to Japan in the 1960s and autos in the 1970s.

As MITI officials insist, developing a computer and semiconductor component industry which can compete in the world market in the 1980s is vital for larger reasons than its own impact on export earnings. The argument goes that such an industry will ensure that Japan has the technology needed to keep on raising industrial productivity faster than its competitors: technology which can be used both to produce and to be incorporated in the goods which Japan sells in the world market, whether they be cash registers, video games, programmable desk-top calculators or disc drives. This is why one leading US expert on Japanese business affairs calls the future of Japan's computer industry 'the central issue of our times'. There is considerable evidence to suggest that the Japanese are in a stronger position to exploit computer technology than any of their competitors in the industrialised West, including the USA.

Japan is well suited to meeting the demands of the market in products which carry a high proportion of advanced electronic components. These markets call for cheap but reliable products, based on volume production using automated methods. Profit margins are low. Launching new products is risky because no one knows what the market wants. Who knew, for instance, that housewives needed electronic calculators? This means gambling on high volume — that is, high investment — before a producer knows what is justified. Another feature of the market is that innovation in production techniques is more important than in product design. As Edward de Bono points out in his recent book, *Opportunities,* the Japanese are experts in conceptualising and hence are able to seek out and develop opportunity.[2] That is to say, they seek out an opportunity before it hits them in the face. They work on an opportunity and develop it, so that when the time comes, they are suddenly found to be dominating a market, from an impregnable position. Seiko did not invent the quartz watch but Seiko saw and developed the opportunity to such an extent that today its worldwide sales are more than double those of its nearest competitor in the field. This 'opportunity-seeking' is in stark contrast to the 'opportunistic' behaviour of US executives. The 'opportunist' tends to wait until an opportunity becomes obvious and then weigh in to try to clean up. This can be costly as, for example, Rockwell found in the calculator market.

Where the Japanese score over their competitors is in their tradition of 'advancement engineering'. Essentially this is an update on Japan's prewar ability to 'imitate' other peoples' products. Whereas there often appears to be a shortage of engineers in the USA or the UK, and in contrast to France with its *grands corps* of engineers from the écoles polytechniques but its weak middle-rung engineers, in Japan there are almost too many. When a complicated piece of machinery is imported into Japan, a crowd of graduate engineers will swarm over it. These seemingly underemployed people will then go away and write twenty or thirty memoranda suggesting often tiny amendments to these Western machines and systems. This process is at the basis of Japan's productivity growth.

The fulcrum of Japanese industrial proficiency is in the general level of competence of the Japanese workforce, which is probably second to none in the world. More Japanese stay at school beyond the age of seventeen than anywhere else in the world. At the same time, for all levels of staff in Japanese corporations, there is continuous on-the-job training. This means that much of Japanese industry is literally 'a factory within a school'. This is why independent experts see the Japanese labour force and cadre of executives as being potentially more receptive to advanced data-processing technology than workforces elsewhere.

But this is not all: Japan has other advantages as well. Given the Japanese system of big business working in harmony with the banks and the government, the Japanese economy tends to much more a 'throughput' economy than a profit-conscious one: at least at the level of the individual business. The Japanese do not measure success in business in short-term measures but look for balance over periods of five to ten years. This is in marked contrast to stock market oriented systems, like the USA and the UK, where investment decisions are dominated by stock market criteria. As we have seen, in modern electronics, an ability to operate virtually against a 'national P&L account' is a distinct advantage where eventual profit is very much a function of hefty volume production, often with 'loss-leading' thrown in during the initial phases.

Last but not least, there is reliability. In the West, the testing of consumer goods tends to be limited to rather ineffectual tests on the final assembled product. In Japan each component is often tested separately. In 1977, for instance, Britain's Sinclair Radionics achieved a notable technical success with its tiny microvision TV, but many of the early sets were returned for quality reasons, a fault which also occured with the company's digital watches. However, the Japanese, who do not operate against short-term P&L constraints, can afford to take more care than their competitors. A recent example occurred in the heartland of the US advanced electronics market. In 1977, the Japanese unexpectedly blitzed the US market with 4K and 16K memory chips, which contain the equivalents of just over 4000 and 16000 transistors on a tiny square of silicon. But what really irked the US companies was that the Japanese offered very high quality chips at competitive prices. It was not that the Japanese chips were better or nominally cheaper, but that they had been so thoroughly tested that their failure rate was significantly lower than US-made components. The reaction amongst US executives was one of simple alarm. They claimed that for them to undertake such thorough testing would bankrupt their companies. They charged the Japanese with absorbing a loss in order to establish a 'beachhead' in the USA.

But then the stakes are huge. The very structure of Japanese society dictates a frantic drive by Japanese industry to keep up the island's export momentum. But this can only be achieved by switching into markets currently out of reach of Japan's Far Eastern competitors. According to in-house estimates at that most Japanese of US corporations, Texas Instruments, the world electronics market could hit sales of $400 billion by 1990. But even if this estimate is too high, electronics will be the world's fifth largest industry behind oil, automobiles, steel and chemicals — each totalling at least $500 billion in annual sales by then. The electronics market looks to be the least susceptible of the big four to overcapacity over the next ten years, and also one of the most likely to provide markets for the high-wage industrialised countries. This is why the battle between the USA and Japan is going to be so fierce, and why by 1978 West European countries were trying belatedly to get into the act. The British, for instance, unveiled an $500 million scheme in 1978 to develop microelectronic capacity and to educate potential end-users about advanced electronic components. Italy also announced a similar scheme. At the same time, British and French companies were doing a variety of joint-product deals with US semiconductor majors.

Pacing microelectronics

Nonetheless, the pace is being set by the Japanese, who in their turn are keeping a wary eye on South Korea, Taiwan, Singapore, Brazil and Argentina. As the world leader in consumer electronic products, the Japanese high command at MITI and giant corporations such as Mitsubishi and Hitachi knows that Japanese industry must beat the Americans in the worldwide computer market to keep its export growth in electronics going as other markets, like autos and ships, fade away. The force of this drive and the US response to it will shape much of business and society throughout the rest of the industrialised world over the next two decades, despite mounting political concern in Europe about the social consequences of the large-scale and widespread use of very low-cost computers in both production processes and end-products.

In the US, an ever-broadening band of businessmen fear that they may not be able to keep pace with the product innovations made possible by modern microelectronics. For example, colour television was pioneered by a US firm, RCA. But US companies were slow to realise the revolutionary impact that transistors and then integrated circuits were going to have. As a result the domestic market was opened up to cheap foreign products incorporating the new component technology. Japanese manufacturers have shown considerable imagination in designing electronic circuit controlled appliances: the bulk of home video recorders sold in the USA are Japanese made, and now the Japanese control half the market in cheap electronic cash registers. A growing band of US businessmen fear that Japan Inc. is poised to do in the 1980s over a broad range of sectors what it did earlier to the US radio, stereo, TV and motorcycle industries.

Whether they like it or not, the industrialised countries are being forced into the postindustrial age. This is because middle-stream technology and work are increasingly moving to the surplus population areas of the world, where labour is cheap. This means that the commonplace products can be — and are being — produced in great volume from an increasing number of countries. At the same time an easy division can no longer be drawn between what can be produced in the simpler and more developed societies. India, for example, not only makes very good standard lathes these days, but Indian villagers put together radios, hi-fi systems and pocket calculators and then carry them to market on their heads.

At the other end of the industrial and technological spectrum (while countries like India and China move towards their industrial revolutions) lies what more and more pundits now term 'the second industrial revolution'. This is the process whereby not only muscle or horsepower is replaced by machine power, but brainpower as well — at least non-creative brainpower. This revolution will transform what is made and how it is made. It will fundamentally alter the type of product that is made and how it is made. It will fundamentally alter the type of work that is available, and how people live in their homes. The technology for this 'second industrial revolution' has been in place for some time. Commercial conditions and the international division of labour have now forced the pace for the widespread application of this technology.

But although a pattern is emerging, its precise contours

remain unclear. In some quarters it is felt that the practical difficulties involved in slotting cheap, distributed computing in wider systems and products may prove obstinate, and that it will be some time before the 'real time' problem of programming microcomputers is satisfactorily solved. At the same time, there is growing disagreement amongst experts about the level of circuit complexity which will in fact satisfy the needs of the bulk of the market. These and other practical issues are discussed in Chapters 4 and 5. Also, despite the obvious pressure in the marketplace from the Japanese, who show every sign of adapting quicker than other less homogeneous societies to the installation and application of the new technology, there are many in the electronic equipment sector (particularly the telecommunications industry) and such sectors as the auto industry (one of the biggest potential markets for advanced electronic components) who see the main focus of the new technology in the consumer markets in appliances and gadgets rather than in industrial controls and office systems for at least the net half decade. Such people argue that the capital investment cycle in many industrialised nations will not reach a sufficient degree of maturity until the late 1980s or 1990s for there to be a large-scale switchover from older mechanical and electromechanical production processes. The office is likely to be transformed faster than the factory. IBM has calculated that the average per capita investment in offices in USA and Europe is $500, whereas it is ten times that amount in the factory.

The Russian lag

There are other major uncertainties which center on the capacity of the USSR and China to present any sort of challenge in the foreseeable future. Much of the impetus to the USA's lead in microelectronics came from military expenditures on components in the 1950s: the US military took over 50 per cent of the semiconductor industry's output. Both China and the USSR (especially the USSR) spend a high proportion of their GDPs on military expenditures, and have done so for the past twenty years. This particularly applies to the USSR. However at this point there is a perhaps vitally significant difference between the USA and the USSR. As the US semiconductor grew in size, there was a need for much more of a 'market-pull' rather than 'invention-pull' approach to the basic electronics business. This meant a major switch in emphasis amongst semiconductor companies from servicing a military customer to supplying mass consumer markets: often markets (as with video games and digital watches) which the component makers themselves virtually created. This massive consumer market in gadgets was simply not available in the USSR. A Western expert working in Moscow, for instance, reckons that by 1978 there were only 25000 computer installations in the USSR compared to over 300000 in the USA, and that while the average American has dealings linked with a computer at least ten times a day, his Soviet counterpart might only have one every six months, if that. Thus, the major difference between the USSR and the USA is that the USSR has headed off the growth of the kind of consumer society which has nurtured the recent rapid growth of the US computer and microelectronics industries. Fully 75 per cent of computer installations in the USA are engaged in commercial operations: everything from writing pay checks to Interflora. In the USSR, not even a Soviet State Bank (reputedly the largest bank in the world) possess a modern computerised check processing and accounting system.

One Western expert, Bohdan Szuprowicz, a Polish born authority on Soviet computers, who advises major US corporations on the subject, estimated that between 1973 and 1978, the Soviet computer industry, which comprises some eighty plants employing over 300000 people, has absorbed funds amounting to some $10 billion. And yet by 1978 the best the Russians could manage was their Ryad range of computers — the best of which is a not very good copy of an IBM 360. By 1978, the top designed Ryad performed only 1.5 million operations a second compared, for instance, to 12 million for

Control Data's Cyber 76, which the Carter administration blocked the Soviets from buying in 1977.

Much of the comparative Soviet computing weakness so far seems to revolve on a backwardness in Soviet microengineering, which is a pointer to why, despite their very real technological achievements, the Russians do not like challenging the West and Japan in the new electronic markets in the near terms. Dr Carl Hammer, of Sperry Univac, which sold Aeroflot (the Russians' state airline) a couple of Univac 1106s in 1975 to handle reservations on international flights, is a close observer of the Russians' electronics scene and has visited many Soviet cybernetic installations. Hammer argues that while the Soviets are nearly equal to the USA in the design construction of computers, they have so far failed to master microminiaturised integrated circuit technology. While engineers in the USA and Japan are able to cram 50000-100000 components onto single slithers of silicon, the Soviets had not managed more than 2000, or had not up until the end of 1978.

It seems that much of the Soviet's technological preeminence has been in rocketry, not electronics, in the defence and space industries. There is little evidence to suggest that Soviet electronics, which was comparatively advanced in the 1950s at the time of Sputnik, has kept up with US developments since then. This was the conclusion of the scientists at NASA watching the Soviet manned flights. The Russians' space modules appeared to them to be clumsy, heavy affairs, with a minimum of electronic equipment or security systems for the astronauts. Further confirmations of the Soviet shortfall in microelectronics seemed to be provided when a Russian defector flew the latest 'foxbat' MIG fighter to Japan in 1976. CIA experts dismantled the plane and found it very deficient in computing equipment in particular and electronic equipment in general.

In the case of China, a report by the congressional Joint Economic Committee, 'The Chinese Economy Post Mao', quotes the Chinese Minister of Machine-building as admitting that the Chinese 'electronics industry has developed into a well-formed new industry; however, our electronics is a relatively weak link. The technical level of products is not high, its production efficiency is low, and it still cannot meet the needs of national defence and the building of the national economy.' At present the Chinese are seeking mass-production technology from Japan for integrated circuits and large-scale integration. In 1978, a delegation of top Chinese scientists visited Britain and inspected both Ferranti (a top UK producer of sophisticated 'custom', as opposed to standard, circuits) and the UK's independent computer manufacturer, ICL. The Joint Economic Committee's report concluded that

> 'China suffers from an extreme technological lag between the state of the art as exhibited in the laboratory-produced electronics equipment and its quality of mass production...electronics production in the main tends to run 10 years or more behind the world state of the art in terms of embodied technology...'

The evidence suggests that both the Soviets and the Chinese are some years away from challenging either the USA or Japan in advanced electronics, at least as embodied in consumer goods. It seems more likely that Taipei, Seoul and Singapore would run both the People's Republic of China and the USSR into the ground in the electronics marketplace in the 1980s, before either could wrest control from the USA and Japan.

Blurred distinctions

A graphic example of the increasingly blurred distinction between zones where it is appropriate to base 'highstream' activities is the case of the Philippines. Top US corporate planners in the computer field see the Philippine Islands as a possible base from which to steal the march on Hong Kong, Singapore and even Japan (perhaps operating via a 'technology transfer' with China) as the electronics war hots up in the international marketplace. The Philippines are seen as a logical site for the Central Pacific computer industry. Some US experts see the emergence of a computer industry there by the mid-1980s. The combination of low-cost labour and a highly educated populace makes Manila an attractive site for establishing both computer sales offices and manufacturing plants to service South-East Asia. Manila wage rates are only about one-third of those of Southern California, and yet there are more graduates per 1000 of population in the Philippines than anywhere outside the USA. In addition, Philippine business executives and technicians usually speak fluent English.

There is little doubt that international economic pressures are forcing the industrialised countries into what has been termed a 'postindustrial' phase and that the business of applying mathematics in products and services will lead, eventually, to a fierce 'proxy' war between the USA, Japan and Western Europe, each applying technology, capital and know-how to low-wage, surplus-population zones. The shape of this may have become relatively clear by the mid-1980s. But it has been hinted at already, by the way in which the semiconductor industry has been shipping circuits for mounting to the Far East, the tentative plans some US computer experts have for the Philippines and the complex of deals which Japan has negotiated with China since early 1978.

Consumers are changing too

Since the Second World War, there has been a shift in consumer behaviour in much of the industrialised world as profound in its way as the growth in manufacturing capacity in the developing countries. This could be upset by an economic recession, which certainly cannot be ruled out between 1979-82, in view of the flattening business cycle and lack of incremental capital investment in the OECD countries since

1974, and, in the longer term, by an accelerating technology transfer between high-wage and surplus-population zones.

Meanwhile, there are definite signs that consumers behave much less mechanically than they used to, or that economists and marketing experts have so far failed to plot new patterns and responses which may be emerging. For instance, in 1973, one of the USA's biggest consumer-oriented companies predicted that consumers would spend much more money than they had in 1972 and that they would also 'trade-up'. This prediction was based on the assumption that personal disposable incomes would rise appreciably. The strategy badly misfired. Consumer incomes did indeed go up, much as expected, but overall spending did not: consumers did not 'trade-up' either. The reason was multiplex, and probably bound up with a crisis in confidence, which is why, instead of spending incremental income, people saved more. But probably it was also based on something more profound.

Over the past decade, fiscal planners in government and market strategists have found that total consumer expenditure and the pattern of demand change in largely unpredictable ways. Governments have found it increasingly difficult in industrialised countries to plot potential tax revenues and the impact of changes in fiscal policy (including proposed changes in increasingly difficult-to-target public sector expenditures). For instance, tax increases have often not reduced final demand in an economy, because, in aggregate, people have simply drawn-down on savings to offset the tax increases. The reverse has happened as well: fiscal stimuli have been neutralised by increased savings. In the UK, for instance, it has been found that a 2-3 percentage point change in the savings ratio (consumer expenditure less personal disposable income) can happen quickly and unpredictably, upsetting government and business forecasts of consumer expenditure in a year by up to $5000 million. As in the USA in 1973, the European experience has been that when people feel uncertain (if, for instance, unemployment is rising and/or inflationary pressures are building up), the aggregate effect is that the savings ratio rises (and fast) to an artificially high level. But this reflects what some market strategists take to be a gradual shift away from crude materialism, the work ethic and loyalty to old institutions. The generation which emerged from schools and universities in the mid to late 1960s has been through what has been termed 'the poverty of affluence'. In virtually all Western countries, real income per capita has doubled since before the Second World War, and in many countries it has tripled or even quadrupled. At the same time, the combination of higher incomes and comprehensive welfare systems has reduced the impact of economic uncertainty and deprivation previously felt by the bulk of the population. This has led to what economists call 'discretionary income' — income over and above what is necessary for the fulfilment of basic needs. The growth of discretionary incomes, coupled with the expansion of higher education, has widened the scope for discretionary social behaviour, and for some of the apparently idiosyncratic turns in mass consumer behaviour, not only in terms of patterns of expenditure but also in terms of how much is spent. Some social commentators have seen the evolution of a social order than celebrates the 'consumers' ethic' instead of the old 'producers' ethic' of frugality, industry and sobriety. But the main factor has been the growth of 'discretionary' income as a cushion against uncertainty and as a trigger for individualistic, impulsive and often unpredictable behaviour by consumers.

New consumer categories

Marketing experts tend to break consumers up into three broad categories: the money-restricted, the inner-directed and the outer-directed.[3] The first tends to subsume the other two, but, because of its main characteristics, knocks out the characteristic associated with them. The money-deprived probably already constitute less than 20 per cent of the adult population of the USA today, and on current trends this percentage is likely to drop to less than 15 per cent by the late 1980s. The main features of this group, aside from low income, are that its average age tends to be higher than those in the other groups and their educational standard lower. This means that they lay most emphasis on survival and security and tend to concentrate on basic needs in their buying habits; staple items with the occasional buying spree.

The 'other-directed' consumers, with 'discretionary incomes', are oriented towards the physical, the tangible, with an eye to appearances and what other people, especially its 'peer group', think. Thus, this group, which probably represents half the adult population in the USA and Western Europe, buys in accordance with established norms.

But some marketing experts see the most dynamic impetus coming from the 'inner-directed' consumers with discretionary income.[4] At present this group probably represents a little less than 15 per cent of the buying population, but it is anticipated that it could grow by 80 per cent per year in the coming decade, and therefore double in that period. This category of consumer, as the title implies, tends to buy to satisfy inner needs and buys in cliques rather than in response to brand norms. This unfolding trend in consumer attitudes and groupings seems particularly responsive to the exploding market in electronic goods, just as the growth in discretionary incomes (and, as a part result, in 'discretionary' social behaviour) seems to fit in with the culture made possible by the switch from and industrial to a postindustrial age.

The case of the home computer

We shall study in more detail later the evolution in the pocket calculator, digital watch, video game and home computer markets. But a brief case study of the home computer will illustrate some of the themes arising from the present analysis.
By 1965, it had become clear that the workings of an entire computer could be put on a single integrated circuit. But no one in the computer industry, largely for commercial reasons, planned ahead or prepared for the drastic changes which

would occur as the price of computers fell from thousands to hundreds of dollars. But then, out of the blue in December 1974, came an announcement from a tiny company operating out of Albuquerque, New Mexico, that it was offering a personal computer kit for $420. The company, MITS, needed 200 orders to break even. In the event there were thousands of orders. MITS has discovered a potentially huge market which no one else had believed to exist. At first, it was largely confined to 'hobbyists', but now it is quickly becoming a major consumer market with annual sales of personal computers expected to reach $3.5 billion by 1982.

We shall be studying the phenomenon of the personal computer in greater detail later on but it is interesting to note at this stage that the 'hobbyist' movement, which has spawned a subindustry of retail computer outlets like Computerland and publishing ventures like the magazine, *Byte,* seems to be a good example of the clique buying by an 'inner-directed' group of consumers. This has sparked a fad in personal computers, which has opened the market up to the peer-group buying of the 'other-directed' group.

At present, the boom in personal computers and computer store franchising in the USA seems to be largely the result of what has been called 'the tradition of the new', and closer to the pressure behind the demand for pocket calculators by housewives, and the family demand for video games, than to a serious demand for computers. Even with digital watches it has been found that a lot of people find it difficult to follow the instruction manuals describing how to 'program' the watches, and in the case of the pocket calculator only a comparatively small number of consumers seem to have used the calculator's powers to work with logarithms.

Cheapest is best

However, one old consumer prejudice has started to erode and this is at the core of the electronic revolution. It is the formerly widespread notion that if something is cheap, it must be bad and unreliable. The point about products with a high circuit content is that the cheaper they are, the better they can be. This, as we shall see when discussing the nature of the semiconductor industry, is the result of the impact of the 'learning curve' on pricing and production.

The key determinant of the pace of the next phase of electronics incorporated in domestic appliances such as microwave ovens, dishwashers, clothes washers and TV and radio receivers will be the ability of the equipment makers brought up in a different engineering tradition to adapt to the demands of the marketplace. So far the semiconductor industry has sold its wares either to the computer manufacturers who know about logic design, or directly to consumers in such markets as calculators, digital watches and video games. This has meant that the semiconductor makers have been able to create and/or feed consumer fads and demands, without running up against the resistance of other manufacturers.

Car consumption

The most notable example of the resistance of a manufacturer has been the automobile industry, which has partly reflected past consumer inertia. Auto designers measure costs in pennies and do not like 'electronic black boxes'. Despite several false starts, Detroit has avoided the new component technology and is only toying with it now because of the legislation controlling exhaust emissions and because of the rising pressures to make vehicles which are economical in their use of fuel.

Until now, US automobile manufacturers have assumed that semiconductor electronics in autos would do nothing to make their product more attractive and, therefore, more competitive. Instead, electronic additions have tended to be made as optional extras from which the manufacturer expects to profit from each calculator sold. But in the USA, in contrast to Europe, individual consumers do not tend to add accessories. He expects his automobile to come fully equipped, and if the manufacturer is unenthusiastic about particular accessories he usually goes along with that judgement. As a result of this relationship between manufacturers and consumers in the USA, there are few vehicle accessory shops. This is not the case in Europe, where car accessories are often added by individual owners and where there has been a considerable market for semiconductors in electronic ignition and for tachometers.

Japanese consumers shape the future

Almost certainly, the most important consumer factor in the electronics field which, because of the increasing pervasiveness of electronics over the next decades, will have a major impact on a wide range of industries operating in the world market, is the technical sophistication of the Japanese consumer. The Japanese are probably the most demanding consumers in the world. They make their US counterparts look like whimsical gimmick hunters. The Japanese do not fall for gimmicks (except possibly in drug buying) which is why, for instance, instamatic cameras have failed to sell in Japan. The country has at least four wide circulation daily newspapers wholly devoted to technical matters, and the Japanese have the highest general degree of technical literacy in the world, which is well reflected in their widespread skill at 'advancement engineering'. Anybody who has observed Japanese shoppers in Electronics City, in the centre of Tokyo, will know just how demanding and informed the Japanese consumer of electronics goods tends to be compared to his US or European counterpart. A major reason why it has proved so hard for exporters to sell in Japan is that the Japanese consumer shows real interest in technology and looks for care over quality. What this pronounced feature of Japanese society means is that Japanese manufacturers find it relatively much easier to sell abroad than they do to service home demand. This will be an important factor in the competitive race for the electronics markets of the 1980s.

For the time being, consumer response to 'computerised' appliances must remain something of a 'black box', with the probable exception of Japan. We have noted how undemanding the US automobile buyer has been so far, when it comes to electronics in the car. But we he also seen how the personal computer market grew fast and unexpectedly from nothing in 1974 to a multibillion dollar market today.

Conclusions

The general and tentative conclusions to emerge from this broad analysis of underlying movements in the international economy and amongst consumers in the industrialised countries are as follows:

- The Japanese, pressured by growing competition from other Far Eastern (and ASEAN) producers, are being forced into a postindustiral phase. The same pressures are also acting on US and European producers. But, unlike the USA and Europe, Japan has a 'technology policy' and is likely methodically to incorporate advanced electronic componentry into its next generation of products by the early 1980s. This will force the pace for the rest of the world's business community, which might well have been slower, otherwise, to use the new technology in place of mechanical and electromechanical components;
- the distinction between the industrialised and the developing world in terms of where relatively 'highstream' activities can be based is fast disappearing. Parts of the US computer industry are already planning to service the South-East Asian market from the Philippines, and advanced developing countries such as Taiwan and South Korea are moving upmarket into advanced electronic componentry. A precursive feature may well be the long-standing process

whereby US circuit builders ship their circuits to Mexico, Malaysia and the Far East for mounting;
- however, for a complex of reasons, both the USSR and China seem to be at least ten years behind the USA and Japan in microelectronic engineering and technology. But Japan may place LSI and possibly VLSI know-how and plant in China to take advantage of wage rates far lower than those of Hong Kong and South Korea, under the combined defence and economic agreements negotiated in 1978 by the two countries;
- consumers in the industrialised world have changed their behaviour in ways which are probably generally amenable to the onset of the pervasive phase in electronics. However in the USA and Europe this may be geared more towards 'gimmick' buying rather than a serious desire to buy distributed and flexible computing power. But, and this may be highly significant, Japan may prove to be different, because Japanese consumers are both technically 'literate' and demanding. This could be an important ingredient in Japan's overall drive to market and master electronic products between now and the mid-1980s.

These factors, taken together, suggest that the background conditions exist either to force or, at least, to encourage electronics into its pervasive phase, over the next five to ten years.

References

1. Blackhurst, Tumlir and Marian, *Trade Liberalisation, Protectionism and Interdependence*, (The GATT, Geneva, 1977).
2. de Bono, Edward, *Opportunities*, Associated Business Programmes, 1978.
3. Bell, Daniel, *The Cultural Contradictions of Capitalism*, Basic books, New York.
4. Shay, Paul, *The Consumer Revolution is Coming*, Marketing, September, 1978.

2 The social and political environment

"First, you have to take the facts, before you can distort 'em."
Mark Twain

"For now sits expectation in the air."
William Shakespeare

The future is here

In 1978, politicians and the public at large in the USA and Western Europe suddenly discovered the 'silicon chip'. But the future was already evident to those who cared to look. It was, and is, well symbolised for instance by the latest generation of 'check-out terminals' at large retail stores. The cashier now operates a computer. This computer not only tallies up the customer's bill, but also carries out automatic credit card checks with bank databanks, updates the store's stock position, instructs a warehouse computer physically to shift inventory when necessary, and monitors the performance, in terms of speed and errors, of the check-out assistant. However, check-out assistants in stores in Copenhagen, Denmark, refused to operate the terminals unless the assistant-monitoring (some would say 'policing') was eliminated from the program. It duly was.

The future can be found too in the office, where word-processing machines can do the job of between three and five typists, and through updated data-transmission technology, can make filing clerks and postmen redundant. In the factory, robots are gradually taking over from human assembly-line workers. In a laboratory near Boston in the USA, a robot has been developed, behind closed doors, which can assemble a car alternator, from standard components, in 2.5 minutes. Through the use of data bases feeding computer-aided designs straight down to the factory floor, via direct programming of NC controls, General Motors is far down the road in experiments with fully-automatic plants based 'on one-man kinetics'.

But highly skilled jobs seem to be on the point of being mechanised too by the use of 'electronic intelligence'. In some US hospitals, automatic consultants, programmed on the instructions of top medical consultants and diagnosticians, are turning diagnosis into a 'Socratic dialogue' between computers and lowly medical officials. The computer comes up with the final diagnosis, after the 'human' medico in the hospital has been confined to asking patients questions and organising laboratory tests at the behest of the computer.

If, as seems very probable, the cheapness and sheer availability of microelectronic devices, and the pressures of the marketplace amongst end-users, force many companies to accept semiconductor electronics as a new 'heartland' technology within the next five to ten years, a host of social problems will arise. Most of these will be focused on unemployment. Many employers now talk of labour as a fixed cost, which must not be taken on or redeployed lightly. Senior managers often imply that 1000 employees represent 1000 headaches. These sentiments, plus the potential pervasiveness of semiconductor devices, mean that design engineers tend to see their primary task as 'designing work out of products'.

The 'job killers'

The English word 'job-killer' is commonly used in Germany to refer to the erosion of traditional jobs in industry and commerce as a result of the growing use of microprocessors. A study by Siemens estimates that by 1990 around 40 per cent of present office work can be carried out by computerised equipment, centred on word processors linked to datatransmission systems. German trade unionists have calculated that this threatens two million out of five million typing and secretarial jobs in Germany. In 1978 the digital watch forced the closure of seventeen Swiss watch manufacturers. Amongst manufacturing companies, Volkswagen had over seventy of its own automatic robots by mid-1978 to carry out dirty work at its Wolfsburg plant. But by common consent the most thorough attempt so far to delineate the social impact of microelectronics has been the already cited French report, *L'Informatisation de la Societe*. The report stresses the need to develop from the 'information revolution' a whole new economic structure based on the recognition of internationally competitive and non-competitive economic sectors. It goes on to suggest that the crucial sector is not just microprocessors and their improved cost performance compared with mainframe computers, minis or human beings, but the combination of computers with telecommunications, satellite technology and broadcasting. These factors together are felt likely to bring about such important gains in productivity that the internationally competitive parts of the economy will diminish in their social significance: mainly, that is, as providers of jobs. The report forecasts that in the longer term this will leave dying megaliths in high-employment manufacturing industry on the one hand unable to compete with the Third World, and on the other, a proliferation of small, innovative, 'highstream' technology companies able to withstand international competition. To provide people with jobs, who cannot be part of the cadre of 'brainworkers' staffing the small, innovative companies, will be a mass of socially-oriented, non-profit-making organisations.[5]

In Britain a report compiled by Iann Barron and Ray Curnow for the Computers, Systems and Electronic Requirements Board of the Department of Industry argued that the use of information technology will eventually directly influence the efficiency of 95 per cent of the economy, whereas support for the industry itself will only affect 5 per cent of the economy.

The report points out that electronics, computing and information technology need to be seen as interrelated aspects of the same basic technology need to be seen as interrelated aspects of the same basic technology need to be seen as interrelated aspects of the same basic technology, which means that it will be pervasive, extending throughout industry and commerce.

The transitional problems are exemplified by the prospects for mechanical engineering in the industrialised world. Without doubt, the introduction of electronic controls will cause a change of direction in much component manufacturing. The cost of the development of advanced electronic components means that basic microprocessors and memory circuits will be purchased from one of the large electronics manufacturers. This will reduce the need for precision engineering and create an alternative need for electronic assembly work. Electronic assembly is lightwork which calls for a dexterity well suited to female assemblers. In addition, the size and the weight of the electronic devices means that there are opportunities to use Far Eastern female assemblers to achieve cost reductions by manufacturing in cheap labour zones like Hong Kong and Taiwan. Indeed this has been underway in semiconductors since the late 1960s. US circuit makers ship the circuits to the Far East for mounting.

The future is a black box

These influences and trends will profoundly affect the industrial structure, performance and attitude of the developed countries, as has been made clear by the French and UK government-sponsored studies already cited. These are not just marginal effects to be reflected in a minor percentage change in the economic indicators. They are potentially deep and widespread and signal a fundamental and probably irreversible change in the lifestyles of industrialised societies. But to try to predict the precise outcome and its timing by extrapolating from the past is methodologically incorrect. By definition, when technological parameters are changing, as they are with the development of solid state electronics (and within that with the changeover from large-scale to very large-scale integration) no known method of prediction (that is, process based on extrapolation) can be used.

An example of a predictive exercise which went very awry occurred in 1949, when the US Department of Commerce predicted that the installation of 100 computers would satisfy US data-processing requirements. In a sense, the prediction was correct. On the basis of the component technology then in place, that of the vacuum tube, computers were very much for use only by people like the scientists and engineers who worked on the atomic bomb, and organizations like the Department of the Census. It took the imaginative brainpower of a Dr John von Neumann to see through the current technological limitations and still christen the electronic computer 'an all-purpose machine'. That is now an apposite description made possible by the quantum leaps in electronic component technology since the late 1940s; first with the crucial invention of the transistor, then the development of the integrated circuit and by the early 1970s with the merging of the digital computer and the integrated circuit with the microprocessor.

But it is still far too early to plot the 'limits' to miniaturisation and the degree of complexity which will be usable. Anyone extrapolating the technology of the 1940s would have come to similar conclusions to the US Department of Commerce, unless he had been tempted to predict substantial improvements in the vacuum tube itself — which would have been wrong. One reason why the transistor was 'unseen' in the 1940s was that there was then no such discipine as 'materials science'. The invention of the transistor required the use of special techniques to prepare highly perfect crystals and the preparation of materials with only a few parts per billion of harmful impurities. This was a precondition of SIC technology.

The exact shape of the technology of the 1980s will depend upon the outcome of research into the use of electron beams to trace out miniature circuits, the development of magnetic-bubble memory semiconductors and superconducting Josephson junctions, three-dimensional information storage, and electronic data-transmission techniques, to mention some main areas of experimentation.

How fast a diffusion rate?

Just how fast 'electronic automation' will take on is a moot point, rather than whether it will catch on. It will be determined by four main factors: the state of the art (which is highly developed); the relative cost *vis-à-vis* other modes (cheap — once the capital investment cycle has matured); the scope of the market (potentially enormous) and the short-term level of end-user demand (this is a variable which cannot be computed at present: viz; the comparative slowness of the auto industry and the telecommunications industry to replace older systems with purely electronic ones). However most experts forecast that the diffusion 'rate' of the technology will accelerate towards the end of the 1980s.

It is perhaps instructive to recollect that a Presidential Commission on Technology suggested in 1966 that

> 'major technological discoveries may wait as long as 14 years before they reach commercial application, even on a small scale, and perhaps another 5 years before their impact on the economy becomes large. It seems safe to conclude that most major technological discoveries which will have significant economic impact within the next decade are already at least in readily identifiable stages of commercial development.'[6]

On that analysis it will be 1985-6 before the microprocessor (and related circuits) makes its impact. The Technology Commission also pointed out that the steam engine and the diesel had coexisted for at least thirty years and that the DC-3 aircraft introduced in the 1930s was still flying in 1966 (and come to that in 1976 as well). It is evident that as the silicon content of a product decreases, as with the auto and the telephone exchange compared with the pocket calculator or the digital watch, electronic components will have to coexist with more robust mechanical and electromechanical parts.

Transitional unemployment

But it seems safe to conclude that the automation of much of industrial production and of clerical work is inevitable. We have already referred to the potential impact of the word-processor in the office and to the Siemens report in Germany and the Nora report in France, both of which foresee radical changes in commerce, finance and office work. Probably 15 to 20 per cent of clerical time is taken up with creating records or transcribing these from manuscript to typed or machine-readable form. A similar amount of time is almost certainly spent on such activities as filing, retrieving, indexing, copying and distributing records. These activities are readily convertible to electronic information storage, retrieval, duplication and transmission as the 'paperless office' approaches, probably in earnest by the late 1980s. This could mean a 30 per cent reduction in clerical effort. This does not in itself entail a reduction in the number of office workers. The impact of electronics automation, or indeed of any type of automation, is on productivity. The number of workers depends on the amount of the firm's business, or the overall level of economic activity in a given economy. It is therefore certainly conceivable (if, as many would argue, improbable), that despite the automation of clerical work, the volume of work may increase sufficiently in a 'knowledge'- or 'information'-based society to create the need for more clerical workers than now exist.

At the same time, the transformation of 'knowledge' work

Table 2.1 Postindustrial societies

	US		UK	
	Employees in manufacturing (millions)	As percentage of total civilian employment (%)	Employees in manufacturing (millions)	As percentage of total civilian employment (%)
1960	16.8	25.5	8.4	38.4
1965	18.1	25.4	8.6	37.1
1970	19.3	24.6	8.3	37.1
1973	20.1	23.8	7.8	34.5
1976	19.0	21.6	7.2	32.1

performed by designers, managers and accountants through the installation of 'distributed' computing may not so much speed up work as make precise the exact operations staff undertake, as well as raise queries as to how these may be combined with other tasks or rearranged in other ways.

While it is too early yet to know whether electronic intelligence will radically reduce the number of jobs available in the long-term, it seems pretty certain that the labour force will be fundamentally transformed during what could be an anguished interim period. It is already happening. In the USA today only just over 20 per cent of the labour force is engaged in manufacturing, while in the UK the percentage has fallen from nearly 40 per cent in 1960 to just over 30 per cent. In France, Germany and Japan the percentages have remained steady at 37 per cent, 27 per cent and 25 per cent respectively. Undoubtedly these proportions will change further, as the number of production workers is likely to fall faster than those in information processing. According to a study (based on Delphi surveys of several hundred scientists and experts) published by the OECD '...owing to the automation of production processes, the industrial labour force may decrease between now (1970) and 1985 by almost half.[7] It should be added, in view of our preambular remarks on this, that it does not have to be wrong just because it is the result of a Delphi 'brainstorming'.

Further uncertainties: the case of AT & T

The exact rate of change is difficult to guage, as we have seen when discussing the factors affecting the diffusing 'rate' of a technology. By mid-1978, for example, the digital watch had forced the closure of seventeen Swiss watch firms. Another example, often cited, has occurred in the cash register industry. With the substitution of mechanical moving parts in cash registers with cheap, reliable microprocessors, National Cash Register reduced its workforce on its manufacturing divisions by more than 50 per cent from 37000 to 18000 in the five years to 1975. In the telephone industry, where purely electronic parts are taking over from electromechanical devices, employment is under pressure too. Western Electric, the manufacturing arm of AT&T, cut its workforce from 39200 to 19000 between 1970 and 1976. We have already suggested what is likely to happen to the mechanical engineering industry in general.

On the assembly lines themselves, machines which may legitimately be called robots may take over many human tasks. Despite persistent problems with 'sensors', robots can assemble autos, spray paint, operate warehouses; remotely-controlled robots can mine coal or operate chemical plant. Robots are already in wide use in the auto industry at Fiat in Turin and Volkswagen at Wolfsburg. The Japanese have spent billions of yen on an industrial robot programme. But neither this nor the development of CNC-controlled ensembles of machine tools means that the automatic factory is the shape of the immediate future.

The basic reason is that full automation involves more than the development and installation of sequential machines. It calls for feedback mechanisms, which sense anomalies in the system, analyse them and take the appropriate corrective action. In most computing circles it is thought that it will be more than a decade before the majority of production processes can be truly automated.

Although the trend line seems clear and the technological

state of the art sufficiently high to warrant large-scale automation, the pace and impact of it will also be determined by the overall level of economic activity in a particular society, the costs of replacing existing production lines and processes (high, and therefore gradual, as for instance, in the case of the auto and telecommunications industries), the prospective growth in the labour market and the general relationship between the cost of labour and the costs of computing. The most discouraging feature from an employment point of view, at least over the next twenty years, is that computing costs continue to fall while labour costs rise yearly, more often than not in real terms, and that the general rate of economic growth in the industrialised world has tended, since the 1960s, to be somewhat slower than the growth of the labour force, especially in the USA and the UK.

But overall it is striking to note in this context that while in the 1960s a 3 per cent unemployment rate was considered 'acceptable' in most industrialised countries, the level of 'acceptability' has probably risen now to more like 6 per cent, or the kind of unemployment rate which became common the latter part of the 1970s in the OECD countries (excluding Germany with its 'guest workers' acting as a cushion and Japan with its system of 'lifetime employment').

Contending views

The most common view on the impact of microelectronics on employment is that what has already happened in the mechanical watch and clock industries in Germany and Switzerland will strike across a broad range of industries as the technology is more widely diffused. The argument goes on to suggest that the job-creating potential of the services sector, which has been the major employment growth area since the Second World War, will be just as badly affected by the new technology as manufacturing industry, and perhaps somewhat sooner in view of long capital replacement cycles in certain industrial sectors.[8] The French government report has suggested that employment in banking and insurance, for instance, would contract by some 30 per cent within the next ten years.

But another viewpoint which arises from this scenario is that far from being a harmful thing, microelectronic-induced unemployment is to be welcomed as it will finally cut the nexus between the question of income and full work of a traditional kind. This approach was strongly argued, twenty years ago, by the inventor of modern cybernetics, Dr Norbert Wiener. A variation on this theme is also suggested by the French report, which poses the prospect of heavily government-subsidised employment in specially created organisations, which will be paid for by the taxable revenues of the computer-intensive, internationally competitive parts of the economy. Something of this theme can already be seen in the policy of deliberate overmanning in the USSR (although the USSR is much more autarkic than most industrialised countries).

There are those who do not accept the inevitability of either mass unemployment or 'sheltered employment'. These people argue that employment in most industrialised countries is 50 per cent greater than it was twenty-five years ago and that at least one-third of all the goods and services on offer in the marketplace had not even been conceived thirty years ago. They also point to other major technological discontinuities, such as the invention of the steam engine (which displaced human muscle) and control tools (like Eli Whitney's 'jigs', which displaced the artisan), which far from contracting employment opportunities greatly expanded them.

For instance, a massive study completed in early 1979 by Arthur D Little, *The Strategic Impact of Intelligent Electronics in the US and Western Europe, 1977-87,* predicts that 400,000 extra jobs could be created in France, West Germany and the UK alone in key sectors, as a result of electronic 'add-ons' or products — such as programmable video-tape recorders, musical door chimes and electronic games — that fulfill a new need without necessarily displacing related items. Indeed, ADL experts suggest that this may be an understatement, in view of extra components and subsystem supplies and service and maintenance activities which will be generated. This, projects ADL, will take place against productivity increases averaging $40 000, a year, per employee, in the four key sectors — automobiles, business communications, industrial controls and consumer products. A recent example of the capaciousness and diversity of the newly emerging markets has arisen with Hewlett-Packard. Previously one of the major instrument makers, Hewlett-Packard has decided not to move into the big market for automatic test equipment, but has gone into computers instead. This leaves more space for others in the instruments market, while scarcely threatening to oversupply the computer market. This is a good example of how very fluid the industrial scene is becoming with the impact of electronics.

The main hope of those who take an 'open-ended' view of the future is that, like the first industrial revolution, the 'computer-information' revolution will create an almost limitless range of new products and services, which will create, in turn, a huge new job market. Whether this *will* happen, and if it does whether it will happen quickly, no one knows, because, as we have already observed, normal methods of prediction carry no methodological integrity as the technological parameters are in the process of changing.

As we suggested earlier those brought up on the older mechanical and electromechanical traditions, like the artisans and craftsmen before them in the eighteenth and nineteenth centuries, should have little confidence in domestic assertions about the shape of the future. A favourite specific example cited by experts who lean towards the 'open-ended' approach, is that it would probably take the entire US female population between the ages of eighteen and forty-five to run the nation's telephone system if it were not computerised: but still Bell employs more people than it did when its first automatic switching service was introduced.

The hidden key: computer simulation

As already indicated, there is a growing body of opinion which sees the key to the future in the 'home' computer and the 'computerised' learning aid in the school. It will probably not be until the 1990s, when the children at present being brought up with calculators and computers become the design engineers and marketing executives, that the shape of the electronic future and the society it will forge will be more evident. It could be then that women will come into their own, since terminal-linked jobs will be possible without disrupting life in the home.

It is increasingly argued that the main social impact of the computer, at least as a system in the home, will not lie in crude data-processing ability but in its central property of simulation. One leading student of artificial intelligence suggests that computers are not so much logical as forthright. This means that they can contain arbitrary descriptions and carry out any conceivable collection of rules, consistent or not. The point is that although a computer is limited by natural laws such as prescribed electron routes through its circuits or a degree of information erosion between input and output, the range of simulations it can perform is bounded only by the limits of the human imagination.

In a computer, objects can be made to travel faster than the speed of light and time can be made to travel in reverse. This is the basis of the view that the spread of 'computer literacy' over the next decade and a half will make current speculations about the shape of the future largely hit-and-miss affairs. This is because, like the development of reading and writing before, the spread of computer 'literacy' will almost certainly make people view the world in a way quite different from the way they had viewed it before, with repercussions that are difficult to predict or control.

Out of all this, it may just be in order to indulge in three speculations about the future — some of the repercussions of which have been briefly noted already: the first arises from the information explosion, the second from the distribution of data-processing and data-transmission facilities to the home and the third from the possible impact of the first and second on political and social decision-making.

The status of information

We have argued that forced by the semiconductor revolution, major technological parameters have changed or are changing. This in turn is reshaping both business and the society within which business operates. The accelerating drive towards distributed computing, made possible by microcomponent technology, is transforming the dissemination and use of information, and the status of information itself. Many business managers have already realised, even if politicians and political theorists have not, that economic realities are far more complex than classical theory would have us believe. Such theorists have tended, according to their political persuasion, to argue either that business creates artificial needs in the marketplace or that it simply responds to the signals of the market. Both sides, whether members of the Mont Pelerin Society or vulgar Marxists, have been caught in the ancient Aristotelian trap of either/or. But once the cybernetic concept of 'feedback' is introduced it becomes clear that entrepreneurs *both* create *and* respond to their markets simultaneoulsy.

Most economists have failed to see this, because they have more or less agreed that the basic 'factors of production' are land, labour and capital. It has followed from this that the conventional wisdom has stressed the limits to business or industrial activity. If one person uses a patch of land, another cannot; if capital is applied to one purpose, it is not available for another; if labour is expended here, that same labour cannot be expended there. From Say and Marshall to Marx and Keynes, it all seemed to make sense. It formed a neat, closed system, a 'zero-sum' game: the more x uses, the less y and the rest have. What these economists did not foresee was the emergence of another factor of production — one which violates all the old rules. This is information. (See also Appendix)

Business managements and entrepreneurs have increasingly found that the traditional 'factors of production', however abundant, are no longer sufficient on their own. Information is necessary too. Information about the market, the political environment, trends in technology, social and even cultural change. Information itself has become a crucial 'factor of production'. This will become appreciably more so as the computer-information revolution gets underway. It explains the background to those arguments which suggest this revolution is as likely to expand job opportunities as it is trigger mass unemployment. It also rubs in the error of trying to predict the future while the parameters are changing.

The main point about information is that, unlike land or labour or capital, it does not get used up. Two entrepreneurs cannot use the same piece of land or the same capital (unless, ironically, it involves computer sharing), but they can (and often do) use the same information. This means that the great 'zero-sum' game has become in part at least a non zero-sum game: This has shattered a fundamental assumption of classical economics, and with it, an ability to predict with any confidence future trends. It returns us to the notion of trying to visualise alternative futures with the aid of computer simulation.

The introduction of information as a crucial factor of production raises some other general points, which are worth briefly considering as they relate to the changing backcloth to industry and commerce. It is now probably true that the 300 years of industrial civilisation, at least in the industrialised world, are nearly over and that there is a move beyond industrialism, which will be technological, but no longer industrial. The original industrial phase involved what has been termed 'a brute force technology'. This made mass production possible through the use of machines which wasted energy and raw materials, and spawned such industries as textiles, auto, steel, rubber and rail. While imposing terrible misery on millions of human beings, it improved the living standards of millions more.

The second industrial revolution

The first industrial revolution was sparked by the invention of mechanical devices such as the steam engine, which multiplied man's muscle power millions of times. However the machines that wove cloth, ran factories or cultivated the land needed distribution systems to be truly useful. So the railroads were built, canals dug and highways constructed. In time, the machines and their distribution systems came to affect almost every aspect of society, from the way in which population was distributed to the kinds of occupation which were available.

The second industrial revolution (the computer-information revolution) has to do with man's brainpower rather than his muscles, and as we have suggested above it is technological rather than industrial by nature. Like the mechanical devices of the industrial phase, 'distributed' computers need communications systems to make them widely effective. With the steady changeover to electronic switching in the telephone exchanges, the development of glass fibre optic wiring and the launching of communications satellites, the world's nervous system is becoming 'digitalised'.

The postindustrial society: corporate structures

The term 'postindustrial society' has been in vogue for more than a decade. Its originator, Harvard sociologist, David Bell, has explained that *postindustrial society* is organised around knowledge, for the purposes of social control and the directing of innovation and change...'[9] On this definition, it is clear that several societies are already postindustrial or at least in the first stages of postindustrialism. When manufacturing is no longer central to shaping the character of a labour force, then a society could be said to be no longer industrial. Already in the USA, more than half the population is not actually engaged in the production of food, clothing, housing, automobiles and other tangible goods.

The next stage on from this could be a move towards a large number of small sub-contracting groups, self-monitoring and self-motivating work groups. The germ of this already exists in Japan, where large companies retain residual employer relationships with subcontractors, so that the livelihoods of the subcontractors do not disappear when another technology underbids them in the marketplace. Another variation on this theme has been the way both the Japanese and the South Koreans have built up their economies. They have both studiously avoided, unlike China, the 'turnkey' route. Instead, their method has been to look around the world for the most advanced technological ways of making anything, and import those ways from the USA or Europe, or in the case of Korea from Japan, on licence; if there seems to be two or even three good ways, then let them compete in the same group. This whole notion of subcontracting and licensing has been used to postulate business corporations comprising in 'confederations of entrepreneurs'. Under this system, individuals or groups within a company could tender to do the work which existing departments are already doing. For instance, internal 'entrepreneurs' could run the typing pool (with word-processors of course) and contract work in as well as out. This operation could become a subsidiary of the main company. The terms of contracts could vary. Some could be almost entirely salaried over the term of the contract; others could involve a small salary, with the rest in the form of equity in the subsidiary company which could be sold either to the 'parent' or to other outside 'entrepreneurs'. Clearly, this 'confederation of entrepreneurs' idea could be extensively used in new end-products and by-products.

The key to whether this happens, and indeed to the type of business structure which does eventually emerge, will be the pace of the computer-information drive and the use to which it is put. A recent US government study has suggested that probably 60 per cent of the USA's breadwinners will be brainworkers by 1990 and, according to another estimate, which underlines again the potential for women, there should be one data terminal for every ten people in the US by 1990. A brainworker can much more easily despatch his work rather than himself to the office. In time the greatest transport revolution may be the telecommunications revolution, because it will enable workers to 'telecommute'. It should be possible greatly to increase productivity — for instance, at staff or board meetings — by doing away with face-to-face meetings round a table with the participants working from folders filled with papers and memos. Once people are used to it, computer-augmented conferences via the television screen will be a far better way of getting a group of people to agree on the design of a product or a marketing strategy. Distance should not prove any problem either as far as cost is concerned. The marginal costs of using satellites do not vary between 'local' and long-distance communicating.

The basic point is that an individual with his own terminal is going to be more valuable than an individual with a file, having to speak hurriedly after somebody else has spoken. Under what has been called computer-aided 'confravision', individual views can be entered on the printout at each person's convenience and printouts and videotapes of the proceedings can be made available to executives not at the conference, so that they can add their own 'input' within the fixed schedule. Far-fetched though this may seem, developments are underway which will make it possible. A number of US companies, like AT&T, IBM, RCA, Xerox, have already put up satellites or are about to; microprocessors have made large-scale data transmission possible in digital form, and the cost of computers is falling the whole time (in 1978 it was possible to buy a whole microcomputer system for around $3000).

A recent study has made some brave guesses about what could emerge from the growth of subcontracting based on cheap computing and multiple telecommunications facilities.[10] It sees the development of a dual economy. On the one hand, the increasingly capital-intensive and automated production of what are in effect capital goods for installation in the household — especially 'simulating' computers. On the other, it postulates an increasing proportion of production being carried out in the informal part of the economy — households, cooperatives, confederations of entrepreneurs and communes. Although this vision of cottage industry is technically possible, it is not probable. For one thing, access to information already far outstrips the motivation to use it. For another, the main reason for the elimination of cottage industry in the past by the factory was to abolish the independence of the craftsman. But some companies are moving some of the way by encouraging their design engineers and D.P. personnel to work, at times, from home terminals.

Political Problems

Wherever the logic of alternative hypotheses about business structure and the organisation of work may lead, the major force outside the pervasiveness and brilliance of the technology, is the power of politics. The major sociological problem created by computer-information technology is that all segmentation breaks down, and a quantum jump in human interaction, even if eventually via 'confravision', takes place. How will society be managed, when all 'insulating spaces' have vanished, and each and every part of the globe becomes accessible to everybody? On the assumption that six hours contact a year is needed to maintain contact with someone who is more than a nodding acquaintance, there is a limit of 720 people with whom each person can have proper personal interaction, and yet the USA is around 2 500 times the suggested optimum size for a Greek polis of 2500 years ago. In this context, and in view of these numbers, what does participation mean and what exactly is human contact?

The sociological issues mean that in the postindustrial society there will be more politics than ever before for the very reason that choice becomes conscious and the decision-making centres more visible. This has led some to the conclusion that tension and conflict will be raised rather than lowered in the postindustrial society.

Not everybody is pessimistic, however. The authors of the French report, *L'Informatisation de la Societe,* cited several times already, see the computer-information revolution as a golden opportunity to increase the dialogue between the administrator and the administered. The report suggested the setting up of a General Delegation of Administrative Reform to rationalise, decentralise and socialise government, working on the basis of information technology.

An interesting example of an attempt to democratise government policy formulation occurred in Sweden in the wake of the OPEC energy crisis of 1973-4. The Swedish authorities needed an energy policy which would lead to a great deal of energy conservation in the country. But they realised that their fellow countrymen would pay little attention to a policy which came from the usual power elite. So the Swedish government decided that anyone willing to spend ten one-hour lessons learning about energy, — how to access solar cells against fast-breeder reactors — would have the right to make formal recommendations to the government. The most important lesson from that exercise was that 80 000 Swedes (the equivalent to 2 million Americans) signed up for the course.

Information

The shape of power relationships between government and governed is not the only kind of power which is becoming an issue. Quite clearly, and increasingly over the next couple of decades, 'information is power'. Whoever possesses information or whoever owns the means of processing, storing and transmitting it, is in a very powerful position. The exact location of this power will not be clear until it is more evident whether data will be transmitted primarily over telephone-controlled wires or whether there will be dominating independent data-transmission systems. But, in the meantime, IBM is a clear favourite as the largest controller of information in the world. With its dominant grip on computing, the company already has effectively conquered half the so-called *telematique* market, at least in business systems. The French report noted soberly that IBM has everything it needs to become one of the world's great controlling powers. This is why there is mounting concern at the lack of progress made so far by the International Standards Organisation (ISO) which is trying to get agreement between the computer manufacturers on a defined 'systems achitecture', into which a set of operating standards can be fitted, so that there can be tight guidelines on how networks can be joined up to permit the free flow of computerised information between different countries and organisations.

By the late 1970s data traffic has started to grow at 10 to 20 per cent a year in Europe and even faster in the USA and Japan. This is why 'open networking' is considered vital to the growth of individual economies. But the main problem is whether the manufacturers, like IBM, will do any more than pay lip service to ISO standards, except in the case of 'low-level protocols', which cover such matters as packet switching at low levels. By persisting in using their own standards, the manufacturers stand a better chance of keeping their share of the market by 'locking' their customers into set ways of operating.

Conclusions

In this chapter, we have tried to introduce some of the issues which are likely to arise for business and for the society in which it operates, as a result of the development of a new 'heartland' technology, based on powerful, microminiaturised electronic circuits. We have seen that this technology, on its own merits, should become pervasive. It has already completely altered the basis of computing. It has made feasible Dr von Neumann's 'all-purpose machine': that is; what has been called 'a box that follows a plan'. The plan can be anything. It can tell the box to turn things on and off, to file and bring back information automatically, to blink lights, simulate conditions arising from the theoretical application of the limits of human imagination. Because of the cheapness and compactness of the basic electronic components, distributed processing and memory can greatly enhance the performance of large host computers or be located where computing power is needed for specific purposes; on an executive's desk, in a machine tool or in a home appliance.

Microelectronics has already created entirely new products with a high microcircuit content, such as television games and viewdata receivers; it has completely replaced other products by substituting electronic for mechanical parts — examples are digital watches and cash registers; and it can partly alter other devices (for example, through timing devices in washing machines and electronic ignition in auto engines). Microelectronics can also be used to counter the imprecision in a mechanical system, as happens with the use of electronic signal processing to remove the harmful effect of tape-speed variation in a video recorder. The list goes on and on.

We have tried to set out the main forecasts which have been made about the broader repercussion of microelectronics, especially when telecommunications and digital computing components are merged (which can happen, and is happening, through microelectronic devices) into a single technological mode. But we have cautioned against trying to predict the future, as prediction lacks methodological integrity when basic parameters are changing.

Perhaps the most salient point of all to emerge is that the future is locked in to the spread of computer 'literacy', which we have argued involves the widespread use of the computer to simulate conditions rather than simply process data. This could result in a whole new range of goods and services (at present, by definition, unpredictable) which could spawn a huge new job market, rather as a replacement of human muscle by steam and the human eye by control 'jigs' did during the first industrial revolution.

References

5. Barron and Curnow, *The Future with Microelectronics*, Frances Pinter.
6. *Technology and the American Economy*, Report of the National Commission on Technology, Automation and Economic Progress, US Government Printing Office, February, 1966.
7. Anderla, Georges, *Information in 1985, A Forecasting Study of Information Needs and Resources*, OECD, Paris, 1973.
8. Hines, Colin, *The Chips are Down*, Earth Resources, London.
9. Bell, Daniel, *The Coming of Postindustrial Society*, Basic Books, New York.
10. Gershuny, I.I., *After Industrial Society?* Macmillan, 1978.

Appendix 2.1
The information explosion

The world's stock of information is compounding at an exponential rate. This is the result of a complex mix of factors:

- the expansion of science;
- the linking of science to new technologies;
- the growing demand for news, entertainment and instrumental kowledge;
- the increase in population;
- greater literacy and more schooling;
- the world 'tie-up' in 'real time' via computer networks — cable, telephone and satellites.

The sheer weight of information to be handled can be illustrated in the following examples:

- during manned space flights, at least 50 kiltobits of data are transmitted each second. This is the equivalent of an *Encyclopaedia Britannica* every minute;
- it has been estimated that even in the rarefied atmosphere of pure mathematics, there are 200000 theorems published each year in mathematical papers and journals;
- a study undertaken by Professor Georges Anderla for the OECD concluded that by 1985, there would be at least 8 million scientific documents in circulation yearly: roughly the equivalent of the entire stock accumulated since the origins of science;[11]

- the 1974 GARP (global atmospheric research project) collected 7000 reels of tape and 14 million bits of data;
- on current trends, and existing current indexing techniques, Yale University Library would need a permanent staff of 6000 by the year 2040 AD to cope with the books and research reports that would be coming annually into the library.

Clearly, the information 'explosion' cannot be handled by present means. It will have to be electronically controlled and transmitted. Between 1970 and 1985, the world's stock of information will have grown in volume between four times (low estimate) and seven times (high estimate). This has led the noted economist Kenneth Boulding to talk of an 'entropy trap' from the weight of unabsorbable information. Boulding suggests that the difficulties of communication and data retrieval might mobilise all available energy.[12] In theory, this problem is becoming as real for managements operating information as a fourth factor of production as for scientists trying to keep up with developments in other disciplines.

On a broad definition, information accounts for nearly 50 per cent of the gross national product in industrialised countries. This is the social background to the growth of *telematics,* which will be the 'heartland' business of the 1980s, just as microelectronics will be the 'heartland' technology. It was estimated by Professor Anderla in his OECD monograph that in terms of numbers and processing capacity, electronic information systems would have to increase one hundredfold to meet the various needs of the knowledge industry between 1973 and 1985-7.

References

11. Anderla, Georges, *Information in 1985,* OECD, Paris, 1973.
12. Boulding, Kenneth, *The Diminishing Returns of Science,* New Scientist, London, March 25, 1971.

Appendix 2.2
Kondratief, Keynes and Electronics

In the CSERB report, *The Future with Microelectronics,* Barron and Curnow suggested that electronics may be a key factor in the second phase of what looks (to the authors) suspiciously like the fourth Kondratief cycle since 1780. Although economists differ over whether these 50-60 year cycles actually exist, and, if they do, the common features shared by each cycle, the Kondratief hypothesis is certainly susceptible to an analysis of the impact of major technological changes on overall economic activity.

According to the Kondratief hypothesis, the fourth cycle started in 1940, having been preceded by three cycles running from 1780-1840, 1840-90 and 1890-1940. Each cycle had started briskly with a general economic upturn, only to move down again at mid-point. Each cycle has had to absorb a major technological change. The steam engine was involved in the first cycle, the railways with the next, the automobile and electric power in the third cycle and electronics this time. Whether or not anything should be read into it, economic growth rates in the industrialised world started to slow appreciably in the late 1960s, after a high growth phase in the 1950s and for most of the 1960s. This fits in with the mid-cycle behaviour in previous cycles. Barron and Curnow suggest that in the absence of changes in the economic order, the impact of electronics will tend to help the second half of the present cycle run true to form.

But this leads to the profounder point, which is the

proper placing of an economy in time, and the real nature of government and business decision-making in a dynamic rather than static environment. This was the essence of the Keynesian revolution, at least on the theoretical plane. The Keynesian breach with classical economics operated at two levels. The first was at the theoretical level and the second was at the practical level of how to use the existing social order and existing economic and financial instruments to counter the effect of an insufficient level of aggregate demand to reduce unemployment to a generally acceptable level.

It was not until a full year after the publication of *The General Theory of Employment* that Keynes himself summed-up the theoretical implications of his analysis. He did so in the February 1937 issue of the *Quarterly Economic Journal*. In that article Keynes explained that the revolution lay in the change from the conception of equilibrium to the conception of history; from the principles of rational choice to the problems of decisions based on guess work or on convention. It had been assumed in classical economics (including, in a sense, Marxist economics) that 'the amounts of the factors of production were given and that the problem was to determine the way in which they would be used and their relative rewards.' This insight could scarcely be more pertinent than it is now. The conventional approach to business decision-making in terms of product visualisation, marketing and production has been invalidated in many sectors by the switch to electronic components and the wide use of information as a fourth and unlimited factor of production. Moreover, likely contours of the future are even more difficult to guess than usual, due to the incalculable effects of such phenomena as a shortage of electronic design engineers and the effect of 'discretionary incomes' on both the pattern and total volume of consumer spending.

Taking as his base point that the existence of money

itself is bound up with uncertainty, for interest-earning assets would always be preferred to cash if this was not the case, Keynes described the way business judgement is actually taken, once algebra and discounted cash flows have been dispensed with.

> 'Knowing that our own individual judgement is worthless, we endeavour to fall back on the judgement of the rest of the world which is perhaps better informed. That is, we endeavour to conform with the behaviour of the majority or the average. The psychology of a society of individuals each of whom is endeavouring to copy the others leads to what we may strictly term a *conventional* judgement... Being based on so flimsy a foundation, it is subject to sudden and violent changes... At all times the vague panic fears and equally vague and unreasoned hopes are not really lulled, and lie but a little way below the surface.'

Thus, Keynes drew a sharp distinction between calculable risks and the uncertainty which arises from a lack of reliable information. Since the future is essentially uncertain, strictly rational behaviour is impossible; a great part of economic life, therefore, is conducted on the basis of accepted conventions. Once it is admitted that an economy exists in time — with history (often misconstrued) going one way and an unknown future going the other — the conception of equilibrium based on the mechanical analogy becomes untenable. As Keynes put it, the deep error of classical economics was 'to try to deal with the present by abstracting from the fact that we know very little about the future.'

But this was not the only major theoretical point Keynes made. He also observed that there is no intrinsic reason why the stock of capital instruments would not become so large that the return on capital instruments would eventually fall so low as to result in what he called 'the euthanasia of the rentier.' This tendency had also been observed by Marx, who had argued that the falling return on capital instruments would lead to 'capitalist eat capitalist.' The incredible fall in computing components adds a fascinating dimension to the argument. It is possible to conceive of a world in which the capital cost of setting-up cottage industries based on cheap computer systems and terminals and easy access to volumes of information about markets, products, surveys, patents, design specifications and so on, would reverse the Marxist thesis of monopoly as the return on capital declines.

However the Marxist point had been elaborated by Thorstein Veblen, especially in his book, *The Theory of Business Enterprise*. Veblen's thesis was that there is an irreconcilable conflict between business and industry. By this, he meant that the essence of business is to keep its products as scarce as possible so as to show the maximum profit. But the drive of industry is to raise the state of the industrial art: to design better products and develop techniques for producing them cheaply and abundantly. Veblen saw a fundamental conflict in the industrial world between the business management and the cadre of engineers and craftsmen. Some might now argue that the semiconductor industry is a good example of a business where there has been a minimum conflict in Veblen's terms. Others may point beyond the semiconductor industry to the broad Japanese emphasis on throughput and sales volume rather than profit, which means that 'advancement engineering' rather than the short-term pressures of the 'bottom-line' tend to dominate.

Arguably, the most pointed example of Veblen's conflict between business and industry has occurred (and it is by no means wholly the company's fault) in the case history of IBM. The computer giant has found it much more profitable to offer comparatively cheap control software with very expensive, technology staid, medium-sized, equipment, than to introduce the latest electronic components into its machines. Veblen's thesis seems to be corroborated by the astounding fact that IBM has managed to run on an annual profit margin of nearly 30 per cent, despite the astounding fall in the general cost of computer hardware. We study the detailed background to this in Chapter Five, where we also examine the case of the IBM engineer, Gene Amadahl, who perceived a Veblenesque conflict, and spawned a multimillion dollar industry as a result.

3 A certain small device: the historical perspective

"we no longer argue about how many angels could be present on the head of a pin, but how many transistors."

James Martin

The engineering continuum

There is nothing essentially new or revolutionary about the development of the microprocessor. Like any other engineering device or tool, the microprocessor is part of a continuum in which each tool has a geneology and is often descended from the tools by which it has itself been constructed. But the microprocessor is probably the best example yet of a machine as defined by the father of cybernetics, Dr Norbert Wiener:

> 'the machine, like the living organism is a device which locally and temporarily seems to resist the general tendency for the increase of entropy. By its ability to make decisions it can produce around it a local zone of organisation in a world whose general tendency is to run down.'

Four traditions

As such, the microprocessor is the result of an intermeshing of three separate, but long-standing engineering traditions and technologies and one much more recent discipline:

- automatic controls and servomechanisms
- digital computers
- miniaturisation
- materials science

Automatic controls

These, essentially, are mechanisms which substitute an algorithm (a decision rule or a program encoded in a computer) for human judgement. An early form of automatic control was developed in Holland around 1650 when pins were fitted to a rotary drum and used for the ringing of the chimes. By 1725, knitting machines in England used cards with holes cut in them to determine the patterns woven into cloth. A precursor of the displacement of the industrial worker by electronic 'intelligence' was the work of Eli Whitney in the early nineteenth century, and its impact on the artisan.

Whitney, who invented the cotton gin, was seeking to organise the mass production of guns. As he watched the clumsy efforts of the workmen, he realised, as he put it, that he had to put his own skill into every untaught hand and 'substitute correct and effective operations of machinery for the skill of the artist which is acquired only after long experience'. To eliminate guesswork by eye, Whitney invented 'jigs', or guides for tools, so that the outline of the product would not be marred by a shaky hand, bad hand/eye coordination or errors of judgement. He went on to make clamps to hold the metal while the guided tool of milling wheels cut it: he made automatic stops to disconnect the tool when the appropriate cut had been made. In the process, Whitney 'invented' the ideas of standardisation and interchangeability of parts, and quantitative methods of production.

Apart from NC controls and 'jigs', there are also feedback mechanisms. The first was put into operation in 1762 by James Brindley. It was an industrial engine powered by steam, with a control gear as a sequential device, which also incorporated proportional actions. This was the first closed loop automatic control. Modern process controllers are a long way from Brindley's device, but they share the same basic characteristic: they embody means for measuring the condition to be controlled, comparing it with the desired value and then automatically taking corrective action to remedy any deviation.[13] This is where computing devices come in. They are fundamental parts of control systems because their speed and information capacity permits a rapid series of responses to a complex environment.

Digital computers

Computers go back at least to 1642 when Blaise Pascal constructed a mechanical adding machine. By 1671, Leibniz had adapted Pascal's machine to perform arithmetic functions. The matter was then left in abeyance until Charles Babbage invented the 'Difference Machine' and then the 'Analytical Engine', which had all the parts required for a general-purpose computer: such as store, sequence control and input and output units, the latter using punched cards. In 1871, Herman Hollerith did something tangible with Babbage's design by using electrical accounting machines in conjunction with punched cards to complete the US population census. He later founded a company which became the nucleus of mighty IBM.

The first fully functional electronic computer was ENIAC (Electronic Numerical Integrator and Computer) designed and built by Eckert and Mauchly in 1945 at the Moore School of Electrical Engineering in the University of Pennsylvania. This giant machine weighed thirty tons and contained 18 000 electronic vacuum tubes (the size of pine cones) and 6000 switches, but it had no gears at all: all the counting was done by electronic pulses. Between 1945-7 John von Neumann at Princeton designed the first electronic version of Babbages's stored program machine. Von Neumann, far ahead of his time, nicknamed his computer 'an all-purpose machine'. Norbert Wiener described the high-speed computer in the early 1950s as 'primarily a logical machine, which confronts different propositions with one another and draws some of their consequences... besides accomplishing mathematical tasks, it will be able to undertake the logical task of channeling a series of orders concerning mathematical operations'.

Computers, therefore, whether they be large mainframe computers, minis or microcomputers, are all machines which obey, step-by-step, instructions stored in a memory within the machine. At the same time, modern computers can modify instructions as information is fed to them, while executing a program. As this has developed, computing devices have approximated to Wiener's basic machines, controlled on the basis of actual rather than expected performance, which is known as feedback. It is at this stage that we are getting closer to the microprocessor and to the point where the notions of automatic controls and servomechanisms are linked to the concept of digital computing.

Miniaturisation

Miniaturisation may well be considered with hindsight to have been the most significant innovation of the last half of the twentieth century; more so than other dramatic items such as TV or the electronic computer.[14] With miniaturisation, quantum jumps in complexity, flexibility and control have been obtained, along with tremendous reductions in size (obviously), cost and use of energy.[15] However, miniaturisation did not begin with the computer, although it is with the digital computer and the electronics associated with it that the most dramatic results have been achieved. The development of electricity after steam power, for instance, achieved marked reductions in size and gains in efficiency. So too did the development of fractional horse power motors, nearly forty years ago. They led to the creation of power tools and small electrical appliances. At the same time, these developments enabled mechanical power transmission systems such as shafting lines supplemented by belts and pulleys, which were very power-intensive, to give way to electrical systems. This meant that each machine could have its own motor; moreover, the transmission loss in the wiring of the factory was small in comparison with the efficiency of the motors themselves.

Since the late 1940s, however, more dramatic developments have taken place. The vacuum tube, which was fragile and generated a tremendous heat, had severely limited the scope for developing computing power for anything outside military or scientific use. This was because once a machine had more than 18 000 or so valve components, it would become impossible to find and then replace all the valves which burnt out. Furthermore, Von Neumann had pointed to the limitations imposed by the size of the machines, which mainly resulted from the fact that each basic component valve had a 'physical volume about a billion times greater than a nerve cell and an energy dissipation about a billion times greater...'. But in 1948, the transistor was invented at the Bell laboratories, by Bardeen, Bratten and Shockley. A transistor is a piece of semiconducting material that uses a filament current and generates much less heat than the vacuum tube or valve, and is also much smaller. But the transistor took some time to replace the valve. It made its first, hesitant, but not altogether successful appearance in hearing aids in the early 1950s, and did not generally replace the valve until the late 1950s. It had such weaknesses as a failure to operate at a temperature of much above that of a warm cup of coffee.[16]

However, by the early 1960s, largely as a result of massive military spending on transistor developments, discrete electronic components were approaching perfection in terms of reliability, size, performance and cost. A failure rate in normal conditions of only one per billion device hours had been achieved. But while the transistor was a vast improvement on the bulky and fragile thermionic valve, the problem of component interconnections remained. The limit in the future changed from being one of size and fragility to one of the sheer individuality of the components.

By the early 1960s the tyranny of numbers had taken over. The computers of the day contained as many as 200 000 separate components. The problem of reliability loomed large again, because no matter how reliable the separate components — and by the early 1960s they were reliable — they were ultimately only as reliable as the joints connecting them. In addition, the generally manual methods used for wiring circuits left a great deal to be desired. A graphic illustration of the problem was the example of the Minuteman missile project in the USA. The interconnection problem was largely overcome in the project by taking extreme care, which bore no relation to commercial cost. Detailed records were kept of each component, vital systems were duplicated and there was endless testing and checking. So much so, that it is estimated that if all military components in the USA had received the same degree of cossetting as those involved in the Minuteman project, the expense would have exceeded the entire US gross domestic product of the day.

As a result of these problems, and what began to resemble overcapacity in the industry supplying discrete electronic components, the concept and then the embodiment of the integrated circuit (IC) was evolved. It was first formulated in 1952 by G.W.A. Dummer of the Royal Research Radar Establishment at Malvern in the UK. Dummer had stressed in a public address in Washington that the next logical step on from the transistor was 'electronic equipment in a solid block with no interconnecting wires.[17] The block may consist of layers of insulating, conducting, rectifying and amplifying materials.' Seven years later, in February 1959, the first patent for an integrated circuit was filed by Jack Kilby of Texas Instruments. The first germanium integrated circuit had been made by Kilby and colleagues in October 1958.

With the introduction of the planar process and photolithographic production techniques, the transistor had largely given way to the silicon-based integrated circuit (SIC) within a few years. Thousands of microminiaturised transistors — the IC — were placed on slivers of silicon each the size of a postage stamp: the so-called 'silicon chip' — or SIC.

Materials science

The invention of the transistor changed the entire basis of electronics, but not solely because of its place in the process of 'miniaturisation'. One reason that the invention of the transistor was 'unseen' in the mid-1940s, and why semiconductor technology had to wait for the invention of the transistor before it could really advance rapidly, was that until the transistor's appearance there was virtually no such thing as 'materials science',[18] although silicon and germanium radar detectors had been used, and attempts made to improve them, during the Second World War. However, the transistor had required the refinement of a technique for preparing materials of less than a few parts per billion of harmful impurities, and the use of techniques to prepare highly perfect crystals. During the 1950s much research was done into materials which would solve problems with transistors of limited frequency response and vulnerability to high temperatures. Experiments were done into such compounds as indium antimonide and gallium arsenide, but the problems associated with achieving exact purity and the costs involved proved daunting. By the late 1950s, it became clear that the future of semiconductors lay with germanium and silicon. The development of materials science and with it, techniques for preparing comparatively pure materials and near perfect crystals, was an essential precondition of advanced microelectronics.

With the long tradition of 'jigs' and servomechanics, the slow development of the digital computer, the development of microminiaturised integrated circuits and the development of materials science, the scientific and technological scene had been set for the development of the microprocessor.

The microprocessor

In 1968, Intel Corp, was set up in Silicon Valley, under the leadership of Robert Noyce, who had resigned as head of Fairchild's semiconductor division, where he had developed the planar process, which has dominated semiconductor production. Intel was set up to exploit the new state of the art of LSI circuitry (that is, ICs containing up to 5000 'logic-gates' or up to 16 000 memory bits).

In 1969, Intel put 'Ted' Hoff, fresh from research at Stanford University, in charge of producing a set of components for programmable desk-top calculators that a Japanese firm planned to put on the market. But the circuitry proposed by the Japanese designers required a large number of SICs, all of them quite expensive. This threatened to tax Intel's design capabilities. The Intel solution, which was largely the work of Hoff and Dr Frederico Faggin, now head of Zilog Corporation, was to place most of the calculator's arithmetic and logic circuitry on one SIC, leaving input and output and programming units on separate SICs. Hoff and his associates at Intel finally concentrated nearly all the elements of a central processing unit (CPU) of a computer on a single silicon chip.

The Intel MPU, or microprocessor, was unveiled in 1971 as a 'microprogrammable computer on a chip'. It contained 2250 microminiaturised transistors on a sliver of silicon slightly less than one-sixth of an inch long and one-eighth of an inch wide; each miniature transistor was the rough equivalent of an ENIAC vacuum tube. In computational power the Intel MPU nearly matched the thirty-ton ENIAC and performed as well as an IBM machine of the early 1960s which cost $30 000 and housed a CPU the size of a large office desk.

The microprocessor turned out to be a neat 'engineering' solution to a design problem which had bedevilled the LSI circuit builders. The problem had been that as the complexity of circuits increased, so did the number of SIC designs. These design costs were proving too heavy for the semiconductor industry, which had had lean years in 1967, 1968 and again in 1971. Moreover, a multimillion dollar effort by the industry to automate LSI design work had proved a costly failure. As a result, LSI circuits only succeeded in applications where the likely sales volume was going to be large enough to offset the costly design work — for example, in calculators and computer memory devices.

Ironically Intel had come up with the solution while

Table 3.1 Number of functional electronic components per circuit, 1960-80

Year	Components per circuit	Technological developments
1960	4	Discrete elements (transistors, resistors)
1962	40	Simple integrated circuits
1965	400	Medium-scale integrated circuits (MSI)
1969	40 000	Large-scale integrated circuits (LSI)
1980	100 000	Very large-scale integrated circuits (VLSI)

designing circuits for a calculator. It had formulated the notion of building a general-purpose computer-on-a-chip, which would be capable of following a program stored in whatever memory was attached to it. This was an alternative to the conventional method of designing an LSI circuit with a fixed design for each application: something which was not feasible if Intel was to meet the requirements of its Japanese client. The key breakthrough with the MPU was that operating instructions could be changed in seconds through the memory circuit, instead of waiting costly months for a custom-designed LSI chip for a new application.

The microprocessor was a considerable engineering achievement on Intel's part, but it remains firmly part of an engineering continuum and within that an electronics continuum, where new products like TV, radio and radar, to take earlier examples, have made older established skills less relevant and forged demands for new products with new capabilities. The microprocessor is the industry's most recent major development, in a technical environment where size and cost per function are falling while reliability and complexity are rising. The reason that the microprocessor is 'revolutionary' is that size, cost and power consumption have all reached the point where the devices are applicable to quite commonplace products. As a result, the development of the microprocessor will have done much more then solve a design problem for LSI circuit builders in the early 1970s; it will also force radical changes in product visualisation, on markets, and on the attitudes of industrial engineers and managers in general. But so too did the invention of Eli Whitney's 'jig', the invention of steam and the changeover from mechanical to electrical power transmission.

Making it usable

However, just to hint at the pervasive power of microelectronics, it is worthwhile tracing the impact of an exploding electronic component technology over the past twenty years on the electronic calculator: a period during which the thermionic valve has given way to the MPU coupled with associated SICs.

An electronic calculator built in the mid to late 1950s would certainly not have been pocket sized. In fact, it would have had to run on thousands of thermionic valves (viz., the ENIAC valve computer) and would have taken up a ten-foot cube. It would have consumed up to forty kilowatts, which would have called for air conditioning where it was being operated. The machine would have cost around $100000 and because of the fragility of its valve components, and the heat generated by them, would have needed continuous maintenance to hunt and replace burnt-out valves. But by the late 1960s, the valve would have been replaced by the much cheaper, smaller and more reliable transistor, which made the electronic calculator possible. But it still cost $4000 and was still the size of a large typewriter. However since the mid-1970s, LSI circuits and the development of the MPU have made possible the pocket calculator which measures in cubic inches rather than cubic feet, and which is sold at the check-out counter of a retail store for as little as $10; moreover, it can run for months on a battery.

This makes visible the power of the microprocessor and its supporting integrated circuits. The merger of the concept of the digital computer with integrated circuit technology has led Intel's Robert Noyce to suggest that 'today's microcomputers, when compared with the computers of the data processing industry, are toddling infants, but their potential is truly awesome'.

References

13. I. Bezier, P.E., *Numerical Control: Mathematics and Applications*, John Wiley, New York.
14. *Understanding Solid State Electronics*, Texas Instruments Learning Center.
15. Hamilton and Howard, *Basic Circuit Engineering*, McGraw-Hill, 1975.
16. Weiner, Charles, *How the Transistor Emerged*, IEEE Spectrum, January, 1973.
17. *Proceedings of the Symposium of the IRE-AIEE-RTMA*, Washington, D.C., May 1952.
18. Petritz, Richard L., *Contributions to Materials Technology to Semiconductor Devices*, Proceeding of IRE, 1962.

4 The microprocessor: scope and prospects

> "any product that uses springs, levers, stepping motors or gears is performing logic and that product should be built of semiconductors"
>
> *Floyd Kvamme*

We saw in Chapter 3 how the microprocessor fits into an engineering continuum, and how it actually emerged as a solution to a design problem with LSI circuits. The strict definition of a microprocessor is an integrated circuit performing the function of the central processor of a digital computer. This is what gives the microprocessor its special charisma. But to understand it, it is necessary to understand the engineering principals of the computer system of which it forms the electronic heart.[19]

Computer engineering

A computer is concerned with the processing of information, which in a digital system (by far the most common type of computer) consists of data in the form of binary digits, or 'bits'. So, in basic engineering terms a computer is a sequential machine, driven by a clock, with a memory for storing data, and input and output devices for passing data into and out of the system. Figure 4.1 puts this graphically. Some of the data stored in the memory constitutes a program of instructions, each of which specifies a particular cycle of operations until the

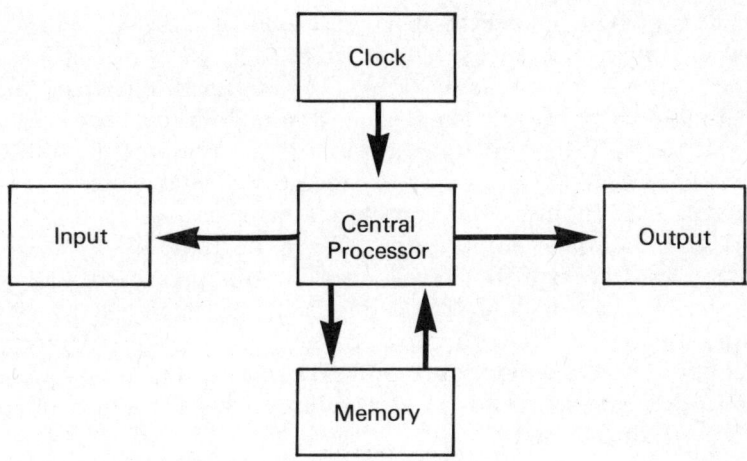

Figure 4.1 The computer

cycle has been completed. The speed of operation is of course important, but more important still is the number of 'bits' which can be processed at the same time. For instance a 16-bit microprocessor results in one of over 65 536 possible operations on a word representing one of the same number of different numbers.

Microprocessor engineering

By linking the technology of the minute integrated circuit to the central core of the digital computer, a device costing a few dollars can contain the processing power of a CPU, which only fifteen years ago was the size of a large office desk. The basic architecture of the microprocessor is shown in Figure 4.2.

Clearly, the microprocessor is much more than an exotic integrated circuit. It is a formidable and potentially ubiquitous control and computing compound. But its significance cannot be assessed apart from the rest of the computing system of which it is the master component. The increasing scale of circuit integration measured either in logic-gates or 'bits' has been increasing dramatically. In memory circuits, for example, the storage capacity had doubled almost every year. By 1978, 16 384-bit memory circuits were common. By 1980, the famous 64-K random access memory device, with 65 536-bit capacity should be in commercial production, even if not installed in larger computers on offer in the market.

By 1978, a typical microprocessor chip measured half a centimeter a side and by adding anything from 10 to 100 similar sized circuits to provide timing, program memory, random access memory and input/output devices, a complete computer system could be assembled on a board not much larger than this page.

The trend has been, without let, towards systems with increased computing capabilities based on fewer and fewer integrated circuits. As the technology shifts from large-scale integration (VLSI) — which takes circuit density beyond the LSI degree of complexity — the distinction between processor memory and interface becomes less clear. By the early 1980s, complete systems should be available on single slivers of silicon with a storage capacities of up to a 16 384-bit memory.

Threats/opportunities

The result of these developments is a basic and irreversible change in the nature of product visualisation and design. But as the scale of integration increases, and as microelectronic devices are volume produced, the problem and the opportunity of investment at large shifts from the cheap, reliable and multisourced hardware, which becomes a commonplace commodity, to the system design and application. But this poses some considerable problems, each of which will be discussed in greater detail in Chapter 6. The main ones are:

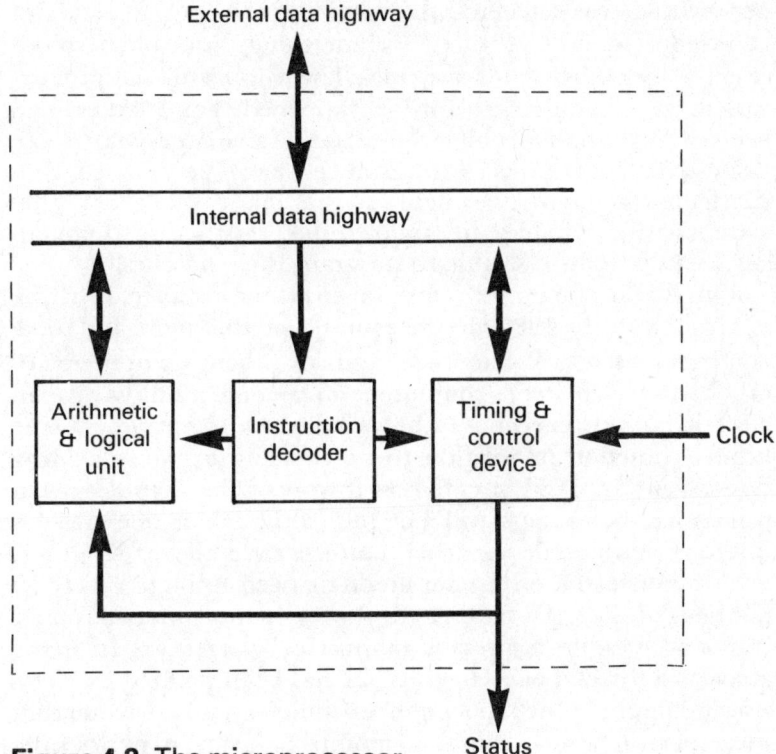

Figure 4.2 The microprocessor

- A shortage of design engineers capable of working with both hardware and software in product design.
- The need for firms without experience even in designing with conventional electronics or logic to design electronic intelligence into their products.
- A slower growth in general programming capability, worldwide, than in hardware and potential applications.

The converse of all this is that the consumer, like the business manager and the design engineer, is largely unfamiliar with devices incorporating electronic 'intelligence'. While the electronic calculator has made visible to most consumers the power of microelectronics, the success of the pocket calculator is little guide to the future. For one thing, none of the producers of calculators had any idea how successful the product would be in the market until it happened. For another, it is evident that most people who possess calculators which can work with logarithms, for instance, have never used that particular facility. It is evident too that many owners of digital watches are unable to follow the instruction manuals sufficiently well to be able to program their watches.

This is why one major computer firm, for instance, is basing its strategy in the 1980s on the assumption that more and more computer users will know less and less about computers. In other words, the home computer will become a utility, like an electric lamp; something to be switched on to carry out some limited function in relation to its capacity by someone who does not understand or care how it works. This does not mean that home computers will not sell, although it does raise a question mark, as do the other matters raised above, about just how sophisticated electronic products need to be to satisfy 95 per cent of the mass market. In short, the potential consumer response, despite a present mania for gadgets, is in many respects a 'black box'. However, as has been pointed out by a leading figure in the semiconductor industry, any product that uses springs, levers, stepping motors or gears is performing logic, and that product should be built of semiconductors. Moreover, logic can be added to products which have been traditionally 'dumb'.

Given the limitations cited above and the fact that microelectronic applications are still in their first phase, it is not possible to predict how far the potential applications of the microprocessor and associated circuits may eventually extend. It has been well said that the virtuosity of the devices will not really become clear until the children at present being brought up with electronic calculators and computers are the design engineers of the 1990s. Nor is it possible to predict with any confidence the time-scale on which these developments will occur. For instance, the application of microcomputing and control to manufacturing industry will be determined by a complex mix between pressures in the world market and the progression of the capital investment cycle. The greatest and most rapid exploitation so far has either been in mass market application, where the circuit content in the total product is relatively high — such as calculators, digital watches or video games — or alternatively in subareas of minicomputing, where the technology is fairly well defined, such as process control or data processing.

The case of autos and the middle ground

An example of an area where the technology has been unexpectedly slow to penetrate has been the US automobile industry where talks about the installation of solid state electronics in the motor engine have been going on since the late 1960s; so far, without much to show for them.

Nonetheless, the middle ground between the extremes of high silicon content mass-market applications in electronic data processing is likely to fill rapidly. By the early 1980s, the estimated market for microprocessor-driven systems should exceed annual sales of $1 billion. Given that most components will not represent even 10 per cent of the total value of the products into which they are designed, this implies widespread applications. According to consultants Creative Strategies of California, the installed microprocessor population in the US was some 60 million by 1978 and will grow thereafter at an annual rate of 20 per cent. By 1983, microprocessor sales, worldwide, are expected to climb to over 100 million units per year, meaning that the value of shipments should rise from 1978's $430 million to $1.3 billion. Robert Noyce of Intel estimates that between 1977 and 1986, the number of electronic functions incorporated into a wide range of products would increase one hundredfold.

The gospel of Noyce

In a now famous article in the *Scientific American,* Noyce set out the case for replacing mechanical and electromechanical components with electronic integrated circuits, although he did not mention the set of problems arising from the lack of design engineering and software capability.

> 'The substitution of microelectronic devices for discrete components reduces costs not only because the devices themselves are cheaper but for a variety of other reasons. First, the integrated circuits contain many of the interconnections that were previously required, and that saves labour and materials. The interconnections of the integrated circuit are much more reliable than solder joints or connectors, which makes for savings in maintenance. Since integrated circuits are much smaller and consume much less power than the components they have displaced, they make savings possible in such support structures as cabinets and racks as well as in power transformers and cooling fans. Less intermediate testing is needed in the course of production because the correct functioning of the complex integrated circuits has already been ensured. Finally, the end user needs to provide less floor space, less operating power and less air conditioning for the equipment. All this by way of saying that even if integrated circuits were only the equivalent in cost to the components they have displaced, other savings would motivate the use of fewer, more complex integrated circuits as they become available.'[20]

But the cost of circuits has fallen: and fallen dramatically. This has been a function of the increasing complexity and the reproducibility of the circuits. In 1960, at the time of the transistor, the simplest functional circuit needed two transistors and other discrete parts and it cost nearly $10. By 1978, with 20000 functions per SIC, the cost had been driven down to less than one cent per function. By 1990, as a result of electron beam circuit-tracing and rising competition in the semiconductor industry itself, a single SIC could contain up to 10 million functions, which might take the cost per function to below 1/100th of a cent.

Table 4.1 lists potential microprocessor applications: the list makes no pretence either to be exhaustive or to have excluded applications which may never be used. Before turning to the list, it is worth bearing in mind that no known method of prediction (that is, a system based on extrapolation of present trends) is feasible when a major parameter is changing — as is happening with the shift from discrete to solid state electronic components. A leading computer strategist in Europe likes to quote the physicist Nils Bohr's comment that 'all prediction is difficult, especially about the future'.

Forecasting flaws

Everyone has his favourite list of successes and failures in forecasting the future. For instance, the successful moon landing by the American astronauts was a major technological project that was forecast with uncanny accuracy. According to NASA, 2329 technological difficulties, many of them involving electronic miniaturisation, had to be overcome before the goal could be achieved. However, such forecasting is rare. Indeed, one of the main lessons over the last few decades has been how often the experts, some of them of the very highest repute, are completely wrong about future developments even in their own fields. Thus, nobel laureates Rutherford and Milliken failed to see how nuclear fission could have any practical consequence. More amazingly, in 1958, a study on global communications by a leading US 'think tank' failed to take communication satellites into account.

These examples have led many to assume the futility of employing technical experts to forecast technological developments and applications. This flies int he face of the current fad for 'brainstorming' via Delphi tests. But the reason for not using technical experts for forecasting (outside normative forecasting like the Apollo project, in which a goal is set and the means to reach it are *then* developed) seem to outweigh the arguments for doing so. The main arguments are as follows:

- Experts and scientists tend to be biased towards their own accomplishments and to doubt whether others can succeed where they have failed.
- The expert is rarely able to balance economic return with the technological advances themselves and their duplication.
- He is usually unfamiliar with the problem of the interaction of technologies and the extraneous factors (economic, political or even cultural) which effect the rate of technological innovation and then diffusion.

Similarly there seem to be strong reasons for not relying on businessmen and business executives to forecast the impact of technological change on industry and commerce:

- Successful forecasting in the industrial field has been rare. The semiconductor makers, for instance, have tended to overestimate the willingness of potential end-users to change their habits, viz., the erratic relationship during the 1970s between the semiconductor industry and the Detroit motor manufacturers, in which the electronics executives failed to understand the difficulties facing Detroit.
- Top management often has an inherent resistance to change. Witness how the US company which pioneered colour TV, RCA, failed to see the impact of first, transistors, and then ICs, and promptly lost much of the home market to Far Eastern producers using the latest component technology.
- There is often a lack of technological data in a given firm combined with a lack of information about current performance.

Table 4.1 Microprocessor applications by sector

Sector	Application	Examples
Consumer Goods	Household domestic Appliances	Central heating Washing machines Ovens Sewing machines Toasters Home computers
	Entertainment products	Television sets Video games Video recorders Hi-fi equipment Electronic toys Electronic pianos
	Personal products	Cameras Calculators Watches Personal computers Pocket tape-recorders

	Cars	Dashboard displays
		Engine control
		  — ignition
		  — exhaust
		  — fuel
		Collision avoidance
		Braking systems
		Diagnostic systems
		Petrol pump control
		Taximeters

Computers and peripherals	Stand-alone computers/ Minicomputers/ microcomputers	
	Memory equipment	Magnetic disk/drum control Semiconductor memories
	Input/output equipment	Keypunch systems 'Intelligent' terminals Point-of-sale terminals and registers Printers/displays Electronic funds transfer Modems

Telecommunications	Data transmission equipment	'Front-end' processors multiplexors
	Exchange equipment	Public and private telephone exchanges
	Transmission equipment	Time-division multiplex transmission telex switching systems
	Subscriber equipment	Viewdata terminals 'Intelligent' telephone receivers Teletypewriters
Office Equipment	Data processing	Desk-top programmable calculators Display terminals
	Word processing	Word and text processor Copiers Facsimile
	Audio equipment	Telephone answering machines Dictation machines
Text, measuring and analytical instruments	Test/analytical instruments	Spectrum analysers Oscilloscopes
	Medical equipment	Ultrasound scanners X-ray scanners Sample analysers
	Automatic test equipment	Microcircuit testers
	Nuclear equipment	Supervising of nuclear reactors
Industrial control	Sequence control	Batch processing control Machine control — machine tools — electroplating — textile machines — welders — materials handling/robotics — mail handling — high volume manufacturing

	Supervisory control	Process plant Transport systems Energy networks
	Monitoring and data recording	Meteorology Radiation monitoring Civil engineering
Defence industries	Military and aerospace	Radar data processing Navigation systems Military communications (scrambling and unscrambling) Guided weapons Air traffic control

- Tight administrative schedules and constant demands to solve immediate problems often militate against the use of sophisticated forecasting techniques in the business firm.

In more general terms there are a number of serious problems in the way of effective forecasting, especially as the rate of change in key areas of technology is accelerating. For instance, even the best forecasts suffer from limitations and shortcomings because of unforeseen discoveries: for example, the integrated circuit, when in 1949 the US Department of Commerce estimated that the installation of 100 computers would satisfy America's electronic data-processing requirements. There is also the problem of unprecedented demands and unpredictable impacts of interacting technologies (for example, the emergence of the microprocessor from the interaction of integrated circuit technology and digital computer central processing).

Table 4.1 shows a range of potential applications. It is deduced from an analysis of the ideal environments in which cheap, miniaturised computers would prove beneficial and within that from an analysis of product characteristics which most obviously call for the application of microelectronic components. First, the environmental features:

- Presence of monitoring surveillance, leading to diagnosis by comparison (remember Wiener's definition of the 'logic machine') which leads to a need for frequent or continuous predetermined or computed responses.
- An environment hostile or alien to human beings (e.g. automobile assembly lines or zones with nuclear equipment).
- Where a quicker response is needed than humans can apply.
- Where a response free from human interference is required; whether misguided, malicious or clumsy.
- Where actuators can be triggered electrically.
- Where operations are repetitive or sequential.
- Where there is a need to supply local information quickly elsewhere (for instance, checking a personal credit rating, transferring funds, or operating in the foreign exchange or money market).

Amongst ideal product features are:

- Volume production, currently incorporating electromechanical controls (e.g. small weighing machines), or where the electronics represents a high proportion of the total product (e.g. pocket calculators and digital watches).
- An existing use of light current and where reductions in space and power can be deployed (e.g. pocket tape recorders).
- Small batch production, currently incorporating specialised control displaceable by digital logic (e.g. 'smart' surveying instruments).
- Products capable of attachment to existing products such as TV, radio, telephone, hi-fi or computer peripherals (e.g. video games, 'digitalised' records, automatic diallers, etc.).

References

19. Barker, H.A., *The Microprocessor in Control,* The Institution of Electrical Engineers, October, 1978.
20. Noyce, Robert, *Microelectronics,* Scientific American, September, 1977.

5 A computer revolution: the computer as a component

> "IBM has everything it needs to become one of the world's great controlling powers."
>
> *The Nora Report*

It is probably true to say that since the mid-1970s the handheld calculator has had more of an impact on the world at large than thirty years of development and use of computers. This is not because computer developments have been unexceptional, quite the reverse, but simply that the calculator developments have been more visible. In a period of five years, the electronic calculator has moved from the world of the engineer and laboratory scientist to that of the housewife and school child and from the specialist supplier to the supermarket. A similar trend is now occuring in computers, especially as the distinction between the more sophisticated programmable calculators and small computers becomes less and less clear.

A computer revolution

To some, the development of the microprocessor in particular and microelectronics in general is essentially a 'computer revolution'.[21] This is the more so, as even very advanced electronic circuits are increasingly reproducible and multisourced. As the component technology moves from LSI to VLSI scales of complexity, the semiconductor makers find that they are no longer supplying millions of relatively simple components to customers who design, manufacture and market complete 'systems' — including computers, defence equipment or telecommunications — but that the circuit components themselves are becoming 'systems', or programmable sequential devices.

Microelectronics has upset one of the established assumptions of computer technology. Traditionally, what mattered were costly switching elements which were kept as few in number as possible. With microelectronics, switching elements have become virtually free cost. In addition, in microminiaturised circuits, switches can act almost simultaneously, while the signals dawdle down the wires at the speed of light. With the microprocessor, a component costing a few dollars can be programmed. In other words, a standard part, capable of large-scale mass production, can operate in a number of roles. This really is von Neumann's 'all-purpose machine'.

Everything merges and disperses

So, as we have already seen, despite their obvious differences, mainframe, mini and microcomputers have a crucial and basic feature in common. They are all machines which obey, step-by-step, a series of instructions which are stored in a memory within the machine. At the same time, these computing devices can modify instructions in response to information fed into them while executing a program. This is why computers can be described, however loosely, as 'intelligent' machines. It also explains why, with their emergence as cheap components in other machines and appliances, they can add electronic 'intelligence' to hitherto 'dumb' pieces of equipment. All this is sometimes lumped together in the phrase 'the smart machine revolution', although, as we argued in Chapter 1, the process of incorporating *algorithms* in equipment has been developing since at least the seventeenth century. The point now is that the microprocessor and associated circuits have made it cheap enough to add automatic electronic intelligence at every single site where simple functions are to be controlled. This is beginning to have a marked impact on computing:

- The computer resource itself is becoming less and less important. The computer is simply one device amongst many and sometimes the least costly as a piece of hardware.
- The focus in computing, therefore, is switching very much from the equipment to the database which it can provide.
- Computing power is being placed outside the central computer areas in sites where information originates and/or is needed, and into end-products to add 'intelligence'. Even the mainframe computer is becoming a 'distributing dataprocessing' system within itself.

The trend towards 'distributed computing', away from large mainframe computers, to the use of separate, but often linked, computers for specific tasks will accelerate as the computer manufacturers, pressed by semiconductor manufacturers moving 'component up' into computer systems, start to incorporate advanced circuitry into their equipment. Even at the time of writing, the vast majority of installed computers (excluding microprocessor installations) are based on medium-scale integrated circuits only.

Information-processing pathologies

This, in fact, is part of the problem. Although the technology is in place and is clearly cheap enough to warrant the installation of hierarchies of computers in industry, both the computer manufacturers and the customers are 'locked in' to middle-sized mainframe computers and the notion of the central computer as a costly piece of equipment which ought to be under the control of the management as a hardware resource and which ought to be used mainly for accounting and payroll functions.

A survey carried out in the early 1970s by US consultants, Kearney, showed that the average computer installation then was being run productively for less than half its available time. The consultants estimated that US business was wasting at least $1000 million a year on computers out of an estimated expenditure of nearly $8000 million. One of the leading US experts on automation, John Diebold, reckons that at least half of the 300 000 US computer installations are a drain on the companies' resources, while throughout the world a substantial proportion of computers are greatly underused or badly used.

The general failure of managements to distinguish between computers as mere machines and the database which they can provide stems from a complex of factors. It has been partially due to what International Business Consultants' Arthur D. Little noted in a recent report as a failure on the computer manufacturers' part to understand the needs of manufacturing industry.[22] It has also resulted from a growing friction since the 1960s between management and data-processing departments. The data-processing people soon acquired a reputation for being 'the great complicators', claiming that something couldn't be done in COBOL, the main programming language used in business.

An IBM executive recently admitted that 'there are a lot of information processing pathologies lying around, which is a hangover from the 1960s, when computers were probably oversold by the manufacturers and couldn't deliver against what had been promised. This was very much the case in product control.' The major snag was that many of the computers had been installed in the 1960s by managements, for reasons of kudos. Most of these managements were unable to counteract the power of the data-processing people who understood the machines.

A touch of 'lock-in'

A broader and more intractable problem has arisen from the tactics of the mainframe computer manufacturers themselves. The first business machine which sold widely was the IBM 1401. The machine was introduced in 1959, and was quickly used for distributed data processing. The slogan 'a 1401 on every floor' was coined. However, this mainly resulted from the primitiveness of the control software, rather than from a positive desire for 'local' processing power. But when the 360 range was introduced in 1965, the '1401 on every floor' syndrome was smartly reversed. The 360s came with a much more sophisticated software package. This led to the power of the central computer area and to what is known in the trade as 'lock-in'. This meant essentially, that once IBM or Burroughs had sorted out the software for a client, which it did comparatively cheaply, that client was not going to put his software at risk by switching to another manufacturer's machine.

Over the years, the mainframe manufacturers have built up huge customer bases. For the most part, these customers have been persuaded to rent expensive and technologically staid machines in return for comparatively cheap software and thorough after-sales service. But this was because the computer manufacturers themselves had been 'locked in' by their own economies of scale and by their swelling rentals.

The economies of scale and overhead allocations which developed through the 1960s dictated the manufacture of middle-sized machines, which incorporated components on the basis of the economies of scale rather than the state of the art. But at the same time, the manufacturers could, and can, scarcely introduce dazzling new machines, while they have such a hefty rump of customers renting staider and less impressive machines. A major effect of this has been to delay the general awareness of the emergence of cheap computing power, based on powerful integrated circuit components. This has led to what computer experts regard as the computer resource rather than the database as the main item in the equation. Nonetheless the mutual 'lock-in' between the computer manufacturer and the client means that the customers, using third and fourth generation machines, running on at best medium-scale integrated circuits, are not going to be quickly appraised of the potential of equipment using LSI or even VLSI microprocessor and associated circuits.

IBM moves

But even IBM cannot forever balk the trend in component technology and its impact on computing. Although the company obviously talks of 'evolution rather than revolution' in computing, the IBM chairman, Frank T. Cary, publicly acknowledged in the spring of 1977 that there 'is a whole new price-performance curve in place' in computing. This reflected not only the boom in mini computers, but also the emergence of 'plug-compatibles'. The 'plug-compatible' was the brilliant invention of an ex-IBM engineer, Gene Amdahl, who perceived two main facts about IBM. First, that the IBM fixed-cost position precluded it from developing the machines which its own laboratory work made possible; and second, that although IBM had been able to operate on the basis of 'lock-in' through the supply of 'software': that 'software', by law (in the USA) had to be made available to all comers.

In 1975, Amdahl formed his own company to make whole computers designed to run on IBM 'software'. But the Amdahl machines (plug-compatibles) were not simply IBM 'copies', they were machines which introduced advanced technology to the consumer faster than IBM, with its overheads position, was able to do. On the back of LSI components, the Amdahl 470, for instance, which 'copied' the IBM 370, was able to offer a 50 per cent capacity increase over the IBM equipment for only 1 per cent extra cost. Amdahl had pioneered a new industry. Itel, a Californian company that arranged the leasing of IBM computers, launched its own IBM 'plug-compatible' in 1976.

At the same time, Amdahl and Itel had technical links with Japanese producers (Fujitsu and Hitachi respectively). This was regarded as particularly ominous in some circles because the Japanese were already moving fast into VLSI electronics in the hope, amongst other things, that they could produce a range of superfast computers in the early 1980s to compete with IBM in the world market.

In the past, IBM has used two main tactics to fend off these challenges. One has been to cut the prices on those parts of a computer being copied by competitors. This has been done with particular success to fend off sales of peripheral equipment. The other tactic has been 'bundling'. This means that the user has to buy a whole package of equipment, instead of choosing what to buy from IBM and what to buy from outside. This has been used with special force with main memory systems. All this has happened against the backcloth of an anti-trust suit against IBM filed in 1969, which still drags on, and wrangles within the EEC, where rulings have been inconsistent.

But the time may be approaching — for a complex of reasons — when IBM will change its stance anyway, due to its perception of the computing market in the 1980s and its increasing difficulty in fending off the competition by deploying its normal tactics of sudden blitzes of new products, price cutting and 'bundling'. The first hint of the future came in January 1979 when IBM announced a powerful and inexpensive 4300 family of control processors to replace the aging low- and medium-range units of the system 370 line.

The main point of balance for IBM is between rendering obsolete existing machines out on rental, which accounts for the lion's share of corporate revenues (about 54 per cent of all IBM machines are rented out in Western Europe and nearly 40 per cent in the USA) and moving the product range into low value-added distributed computing systems.

It's all database

As IBM and the other mainframe manufacturers adjust to the pressures from microelectronic components, the notion of the database made possible by 'on-site' computing and efficient data transmission is beginning to be more widely understood. This was graphically illustrated by the Arthur D. Little report cited above. For example, it has been found from a long-term study of automated industry that the main cause of inefficiency in manufacturing industry is the amount of 'idle time' spent by materials and parts in the factory. According to ADL this can often amount to 98.5 per cent of the time and materials spent in the factory, since of the 5 per cent of the factory time a material spends, on average, on the machine tool, only 30 per cent of that is productive. In this area alone, cheap, distributed computing could have a sizeable impact by enabling the factory manager not only to have a 'real time' description of exactly where materials are, and what has been done to them, but also to see the plant in overall process terms rather than in separate compartments. A possible data architecture, based on distributed computers, is easy to outline. The first stage is to capture the data about a material in process, where possible, on the machine tool. There may already be a small computer on the tool in the form of a numerical control.

The next stop in the 'systems' approach would be to have this computer linked to one central computer. The aim, then, would be to install small computers at each of the separate cost centres in a factory, so that the foreman in charge of, say, the turning shop would control information from each of the lathes under his charge. The next stop would be to link them all up so that the factory manager would have a 'real time' profile of the progress on each job-route-card and the location and state of each component and part in the factory. He would also be in a position to simulate on his computer the plant's prospective response to different potential decisions about schedules or changed orders of priority.

This is what has led one expert to term the database — the information a manager has on tap in 'real time' about his business — a 'fourth factor of production' along with land, labour and capital. Moreover, the database can be used as a link between product design and the production cycle. By the late 1970s, computer-aided design was so well advanced in such factors as textiles, shoes, packaging, the process industries and electronics (circuit boards and integrated circuits) that the design could be directly linked to the production process by computer. In short the design fed into the database could be used to drive the production equipment.[23] Although, on the whole, industries where two-dimensional designs and light materials applied were more adaptable to this process, the aerospace and auto industries had experimented successfully with advanced systems of this kind.

All this is made possible by 'located' computing and data architecture involving a hierarchy of computers, from large mainframes, down to microcontrols, based on advanced microelectronics. This architecture includes equipment not hitherto regarded as computer hardware. For instance, the terminal which used to function simply as input transmitter from the operator to the CPU of the computer and displayed outputs on a screen, can now carry out some preliminary and independent processing on the operator's input before communication with the CPU, if it has one or two microprocessors at work within it. Similarly, word processing has been growing in recent years as a result of microprocessors. A $10 000 word processor can replace a typist. By reducing the typing to high-speed input of raw text with added facilities for layout design and error correction, 'computing power' has been added to conventional typing. This has not only raised typing productivity by an estimated 200 per cent, but the quality of executive reports has been improved because of the facilities of easy correction offered to the author.

Distributed DP in sum

In sum, the main advantages of distributed data processing (DP) made possible by microelectronics are as follows:

- Since many elements of a computer can be working on different portions of the same task, the work can be done faster.
- A network becomes relatively immune to the malfunctioning of one element, because workloads can be shifted or shared within the system.
- A network can be small enough to be contained in a single laboratory or it can spread across a wide area, as between the branches of an insurance company.
- Terminals can include TV and radio receivers and telephones.

The first two advantages listed above lead to the unexpected point that distributed processing is not just something which can be apportioned between different machines or separated machine components, but can be used to improve the performance of a single mainframe computer. We have seen how the large mainframe manufacturers are precluded by their economies of scale and by their huge rental bases from incorporating a whole series of advanced circuits into their designs. But the widespread use of 'distributed processing' within a mainframe system itself would not only provide the actuarial points cited above, but would also solve problems in such key areas as portable software.

Telematics

Potentially, the most important development of all in data processing is the merger of teleprocessing and telecommunications into a single technological mode.[24] As computers become used more and more as switching devices in communications networks, and while electronic communications facilities become intrinsic elements in computer data-processing services, the distinction between processing and transmission becomes indistinguishable. The difference between operating on data so as to make it more useful for the end-user and transmitting it from A and B in the most useable form is fuzzy.

This merger is due to microelectronics. Low cost, reliability and compactness are crucial to communications systems, particularly those involving satellites or spacecraft. As increasing numbers of circuit elements are fabricated on silicon chips, the cost of the basic circuit function deteriorates markedly, as we have already seen. In communications, for instance, a circuit of great significance is the 'logic-gate'. This controls the flow of information, providing an output signal only when the input signals are in the prescribed states. Hence the 'logic-gate' is a basic element in digital signal processing.

It is estimated that the progression of the logic-gate from a device consisting of vacuum tubes to an integrated circuit consisting of thousands of gates has increased the reliability of the device by a factor of 100000 and brought the cost down from nearly $10 to under 1 cent. At the same time, the switching machines which control the routing of telephone calls have benefited enormously from the explosive developments in microelectronics. An electronic processor, consisting mostly of an LSI central control circuit and components that store data, can handle up to 100000 telephone calls simultaneously as well as cope with such chores as diagnosing faults and failed circuits. The objective set for these devices is that they should have no more than two hours 'downtime' in forty years operating life.

A dramatic application of microtechnology has been time-assignment-speech-interpolation (TASI). This concept, originally developed at the Bell Laboratories, exploits the brief silences in ordinary conversations to take a channel away from a speaker who is pausing momentarily and assign it to someone who is speaking. The juggling is so rapid and accurate that the speakers are unaware of it. The technique can now be used to convert a large number of voice signals into digits, so as to reduce considerably the effective 'bit' rate per voice channel. Add such devices as microelectronic stored program controls and random access memory circuits to 'logic-gates' and switching machines, and it can be seen that telephones, radios and TV receivers can be transformed from 'dumb' terminals into positive parts of a network, rather as the conventional computer terminal has been brought on stream as a local data processor. The telephone, for instance, will be able amongst other things, to handle cash transactions, automatically dial numbers and reroute calls to alternative numbers.

The French have termed the result of this use of common components for data processing and data transmission, *telematic* or *telematique*. It becomes clear that silicon circuits are to the emerging industrial phase what steel was to the first industrial revolution and that the development of sophisticated data-transmission systems is to the computer revolution what road, rail and canal were to manufacturing industry in the nineteenth century. The following are the five main areas which will be affected by *telematics:*

- The 'merging' of telephone and computer systems and of telecommunications and teleprocessing into a single technological mode. This will lead to the problem of whether transmission will go primarily over telephone-controlled wires, or whether there will be independent data-transmission systems. This will lead to the subquestion of the relative use of microwave relay, satellite transmission (this seems to be where IBM is placing its bets), and coaxial cables or glass fibre wires as transmission systems.
- The substitution of electronic for paper processing. This includes electronic banking to eliminate the use of checks; the electronic delivery of the mail; facsimile rather than postal delivery.
- The expansion of TV, through cable systems, to allow for multiple channels and specialised services and the linkage of home terminals to local or central stations, so that the person at home can directly communicate with suppliers of services

via his TV receiver. The stations may well be communications satellites offering TV programmes or 'yellow pages' for the subscriber.
* The reorganisation of information storage and retrieval systems, based on the computer, to allow for interactive network communication in team research, entrepreneurial cooperatives, and direct retrieval from data banks to library or home terminals.

The impact of gadget computing

We have already mentioned the blurred distinction between programmable calculators and fully-fledged home computers. The home computer market is growing fast, and has quickly moved beyond the 'hobbyist' market which it remained for several years after MITS had put the first personal computer on the market at the tail end of 1974. But the notion of the home computer does not only spring from the electronic calculator. Many are extensions of TV games. Just as the pocket calculator sold much more widely than had been expected and the first suppliers were small companies, so with personal computers, it is only now that big companies like Texas Instruments are stepping into the marketplace with their products.

Nonetheless, there is little agreement on the impact of the widespread installation of home computers on computing in general. Some argue that house computers will boost the drive to cheapen 'software', either through 'hardware' programming modules and/or the extension of programming abilities well beyond professional DP personnel. It is hoped that as more and more children are brought up with computers, a number of information-processing pathologies will dissolve. There are also those who hope that the widespread use of home computers will encourage the development of the main social property of the computer — its ability to simulate — and that this will be more widely recognised and exploited. One leading student of

Table 5.1 Evolution of computers, five generations

Generation	Date introduced	Speed (memory and processor) in seconds	Number of instructions	On-line file in bits
First	1951-2	10^{-3}	<100	10^7
Second	1958-60	10^{-5}	≈ 100	10^9
Third	1963-5	$<10^{-6}$	≈ 200	10^{11}
Fourth	1969-72	10^{-7}	>200	10^{13}
Fifth	1980(?)	10^{-8}	many thousands	10^{15}

artificial intelligence has argued that computers are not so much logical as forthright. This means that computers can contain arbitrary descriptions and carry out any conceivable collection of rules, consistent or not. The point is that the range of computer simulations is as wide as the bounds of the human imagination. Computer simulations are physically limited only by natural laws governing such matters as possible electron routes through circuits and the minimum degree of information erosion between input and output. To some, this opens up the prospect of new art forms and varied cottage industries centred on the home-based design of products and services.

But not everyone agrees. One major computer manufacturer, as we have already noted, is basing its strategy into the 1980s on the assumption that although distributed data processing and home computing are trends which are alive and

Basic hardware	Design components	Software	Uses
thermionic valves	standard electric	machine language	the sciences
transistors	logic-gates	Cobol, Algol, Fortran	data processing in business (accounts or finance)
integrated circuits (IC)	multiple circuits	multi-programming	information processing (sorting out vast data into manageable information)
medium-scale IC-50-200 logic-gates	subcomputer functions	conversational systems	on-line information processing
large-scale IC — several thousand logic gates	computer functions (semiconductor memories and processors)	hardware programs: natural language	'intelligent' machines as a 'real time' aid to man

well, computers will be regarded more and more as utilities as they are more widely installed. It is already evident, as we have mentioned before, that the mass of consumers is probably more prepared for gadgets than computerised products. For instance it has been noticed that many consumers are disinclined to replace their conventional stereo systems with complex 'digital' systems. On this argument computer-users will know less and less about them. The computer, like the electric lamp, may well become something which is switched on to carry out some very limited function (such as display next week's appointments) but which the user himself will know very little about.

At the same time, computers are mostly appearing in the schools in computer-aided instruction and not as machines to be broken down and understood. In other words, there has been little emphasis on teaching children about computers, only on using computers to help teach them about other things.

Conclusions

Notwithstanding the uncertainties noted in this chapter, the computer is definitely being radically changed by the development of ever cheaper and more reliable microelectronic circuits; which themselves can no contain entire computers, but not of course, entire computer systems. We may recapitulate the areas of change as follows:

- Computers need no longer be large and costly machines, built up from thousands of components. They are increasingly becoming cheap, compact devices, which can be located outside the central computer area to sites where information originates and/or is needed. This is forcing a shift of focus away from the hardware to the database which computers can provide and to problems associated with programming and applications.
- At the same time, the cheapness of microprocessor-driven computer systems means that 'dedicated' controls can be placed quite literally wherever even the simplest controls are needed.
- The move to distributed data processing involves the transformation of hitherto 'dumb' devices — such as computer terminals, word and text machines, telephones, facsimile machines and TV and radio receivers — into computers able to process data independently before putting it back into the network.
- The distinction between data transmission — whether signalled or printed — and data processing is disappearing as each is increasingly based on the same types of circuits — 'logic-gates', random access and stored memory, and microprocessor circuits.

- The distinction too between 'intelligent' terminals and receivers, programmable calculators, video games and fully-fledged small personal computers is disappearing too, and almost certainly 'home' computers will be widely installed over the next decade: but this may turn the comptuer into a utility rather than help develop one of its main social functions, which is simulation.

But while the component technology is sufficiently advanced to achieve the move to very widely distributed computing, resembling an almost Darwinian formation of computer species tailored to different environments and functions, within rapid and accurate communications networks, there are plenty of potential difficulties arising from software and applications. These are likely to be serious limiting factors over the next half decade.

References

21. Barron & Curnow, *The Future with Microelectronics,* Frances Pinter, 1979.
22. *The Strategic Impact of Intelligent Electronics in the United States and Western Europe, 1977-1987,* Arthur D. Little Ltd.
23. Orme, M., *Shopfloor Computers,* Engineering Today, February, 1978.
24. *L'Informatisation de la Societe, Documentation Francaises,* 1978.

6 The human engineering problem: limits on the future

"the user always has the problem of figuring out what to do with our components."

Bernard H. List

"On its own a microprocessor is useless, except maybe as a tie-pin."

Jerry Wasserman

The new computing power is increasingly volume produced, and multisourced (especially as the Japanese manufacturers enter the market) by a highly competitive semiconductor industry. This means that advanced electronic components have to be regarded as a radically new commodity. Unlike the materials or basic components of old, the microelectronic component is the result of 'highstream technology', comes from the most developed economies and is packaged in a most sophisticated way. But it is an increasingly standardised raw component. This presents both a threat and an opportunity to end-users, who must add ingenuity and ideas for applications to take advantage of the advanced componentry.

Already, there is a growing fear amongst many US and European businessmen that they may not be able to keep abreast with the product developments made possible by modern electronics. It is widely felt that Japanese industry will be quicker effectively to install electronic components in a wide range of end-products than their US and European competitors. An often cited example is that colour TV was pioneered by a US company, RCA. But, on the whole, US companies, including RCA, were slow to appreciate the impact of transistors and then of integrated circuits on TV design and manufacture. As a result, the US domestic TV market was opened up to cheap foreign products, incorporating the latest technology. The Japanese, who as we shall see in the next chapter are developing their own VLSI capacity, have shown considerable imagination in designing electronic circuit-controlled appliances. For instance, the bulk of video recorders sold in the USA and Europe were Japanese-made by the late 1970s. Another example was the swift control by 1978 of Japanese manufacturers over the US market in cheap electronic cash registers.

The digital timepiece vibrates the future

The digital watch has been a notable example of the way in which advanced circuitry can transform a whole industry. Digital watches were the creation of the semiconductor industry itself. The basic system was simple enough. A battery causes a quartz crystal to vibrate: an integrated circuit counts the vibrations into clock seconds and then instructs the display system to display the time graphically on the watch face. By 1980, digital watch sales are expected to represent around 40 per cent of total world timepiece sales according to Mackintosh Consultants. Under the powerful drive of producers like Seiko and Texas Instruments, the quartz watch may well take well over 50 per cent of world watch sales by 1985 and up to two-thirds of clock sales by then. In 1976, digital watches had only 12 per cent of the market and electronic clocks had only 6 per cent.

The timepiece market has not only demonstrated the power of the electronic industry to transform a whole end-user industry within the space of a few years, but is also an early example of the danger of myopia amongst producers using older mechanical and electromechanical products in their products. As late as February 1978, when the digital watch had clearly shown its growing power in the marketplace, a major Swiss manufacturer commented that 'Switzerland's policy for the next five years in watch design would be to concentrate on the production of the mechanical watch'. But by the end of that year, seventeen major Swiss watch-makers had gone out of business, and, in the old established clock industry in South-West Germany, employment had been cut form 32000 to 18000 between early 1970 and 1978, because of competition from electronic timepieces.

Not just myopia

But myopia is only one amongst several potential problems confronting business managements as microelectronics moves into what has been termed its 'pervasive phase'. The main problem areas are:

- The need for managements, often currently underusing or using badly their existing third or fourth generation computer resource, to learn how to manage and control a database formed out of a 'distributed data-processing system'.
- The shortage of design engineers who can design 'electronic intelligence' into process and products.[25] This presents an added problem for businesses marketing products which do not even incorporate mechanical or electromechanical controls at present.
- The overall shortage of programming capability in relation to the rapidly growing population of installed computers (mainframe, mini and micro) and the scarcity within that of programmers capable of devising machine codes for microsystems.

We have already described in detail the trend towards 'distributed processing' made possible by the development of cheap, complex circuit components. We have seen how 'intelligent' terminals, machine controls and word processors are poised to change the face of the factory and the office. What it means in essence for management is that the database becomes the major asset — not the hardware that makes the database possible. The computers and terminals, made cheaper by the electronics 'learning curve', are quickly becoming just other machines and pieces of equipment.

Managers must change too

Managements will need to wean themselves of the notion of the central computer area and be prepared to install 'user-driven' systems, such as that outlined in the Arthur D. Little report cited in previous chapters. This will call for a commitment from the top management down. The basic point is that once a microprocessor-driven control is installed, it follows that sophisticated controls are available at virtually the same cost as crude controls. It is thus possible at marginal expense to increase the functional complexity of the control system by a large factor. In both the office and the factory the acquisition (or lease) of equipment, whether 'intelligent' terminals, word processors, or automation and data capture equipment, can be easily purchased by the end-user and not, as previously, by the computer department, central management services or the equivalent. The individual design engineer, for instance, has no difficulty in buying a $3000 microcomputer system without reference to the DP department or central management services. It follows from this that the role of the central authority within an organisation is radically changed. In other words, the centre cannot expect to control information by merely handling the control of the selection and purchase of computing equipment.

The implications for the central management services, and for the top management are very great. Computing is no longer a naturally centralised activity, as managements have been 'programmed' to believe during the last fifteen years, since the introduction of the IBM 360 range of large host computers, with sophisticated control software calling for powerful DP departments. The individual items of hardware are now becoming too low in cost to allow standards to be maintained through the traditional budgetary authority within an organisation. But new standards of interlinking will become more necessary as the handling and storage of information become more widespread and dispersed. In short, if central management services are to continue to exercise their traditional control, they must shift their focus from the computer resource to the database: they must control communications rather than attempt to control all purchasing policy: they must ensure that the systems are 'user-driven' by the line-management and that top management knows how to use 'cross-file' computer systems. Unless this happens, there is the danger of 'information anarchy', which would simply provide work for bigger mainframe computers in analysing and storing away the data as well as added power for the DP department. But as yet there is little evidence that most managements are aware of these matters; the imminent need for changes in management styles — dictated by the transformation of data processing and data transmission — calls for managements to study for themselves the principles of control theory.

This also means, as we have already suggested, that managements should cease to regard the computer as equipment to be used for accounting and financial tasks to the exclusion of most other functions. The computer hierarchy should act as a nerve network carrying information for each part of the system. Figure 6.1 suggests an organisation structure for a manufacturing company, known as the Crawford Structure.

These matters obviously highlight the need for managers to dispense with old ways. The main lessons in process and product development for managers are:

- That they should become informed on the scope and cost of using microprocessors, and of the trends, even if it means hiring a consultant. What may not be feasible today may be feasible very soon, and may be exploited by a competitor — so fast is the fall in microelectronic component prices.

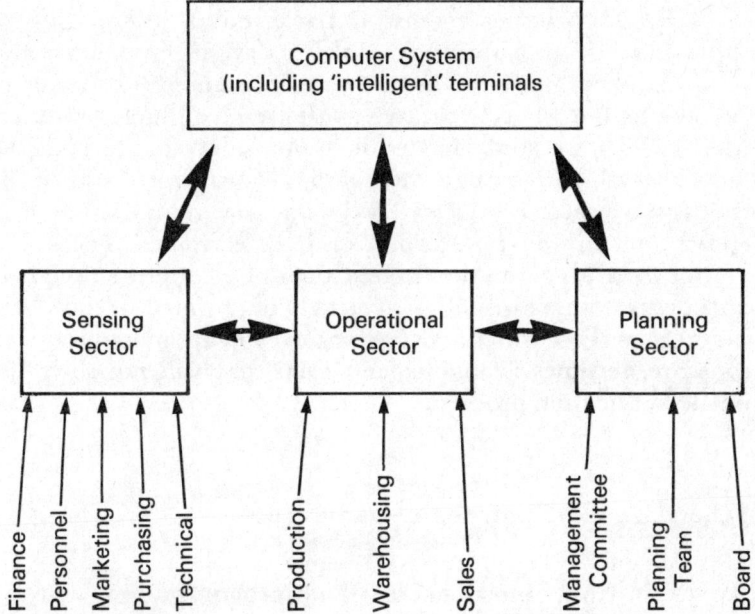

Figure 6.1 The Crawford structure, computerised business organisation

- To make sure that those responsible for product planning are even better informed than they are and that they have access to equipment and technology as required. As we have already seen, the computer system as a hierarchy of bits and pieces of hardware is now relatively unimportant in itself and cheap. A more difficult lesson, as we shall show in the next section of this chapter, is that management must try to make sure that the software skills are available within the organisation, or that they are made available from specialist companies.
- Most of all, perhaps, there is a need to stay receptive to new ideas, whether they apply to existing business activities or to new ventures. Microelectronics is not only transforming existing products, as with the timepiece or the oven, but is also creating completely new products, such as video games.

These are truisms against a background where, due to shortages of appropriately skilled design engineers and programmers, much of industry and commerce is going to become as fiercely competitive as the semiconductor industry itself (which we study in detail in the next chapter). These 'bottlenecks', rather than the myopia shown, for instance, by the Swiss watch industry, will be the main short-term constraints on the application of microelectronics. Those who do not have access to the limited pool of electronics designers and programmers will be increasingly outgunned in the world markets by those who do, unless or until cheap, mass-produced software becomes available: and even that will not solve the whole application problem.

Where are the design engineers?

By definition, most users of microcomputers will be unsophisticated users, unless or until computer 'literacy' spreads far beyond the DP department. This remains an even worse problem while micros themselves are both difficult to program and connect to other things. At the moment, during the first phase of the microelectronic revolution, products incorporating electronic intelligence are coming into markets where many of the manufacturers have not even had experience with conventional electronics; much less with designing electronic brains into their products. Throughout the 1970s, a gulf has widened between the semiconductor makers and much of the rest of industry. Even in 1977, a leading consultant was suggesting that the technology remained five years ahead of potential applications. The gap may have started to close, but only because the semiconductor makers have been forced to realise that they are not just selling hardware but 'systems'.

The root problem for many corporations, large and small, is a shortage of design engineers with the requisite skills to use microprocessors and computers in product design. This will be

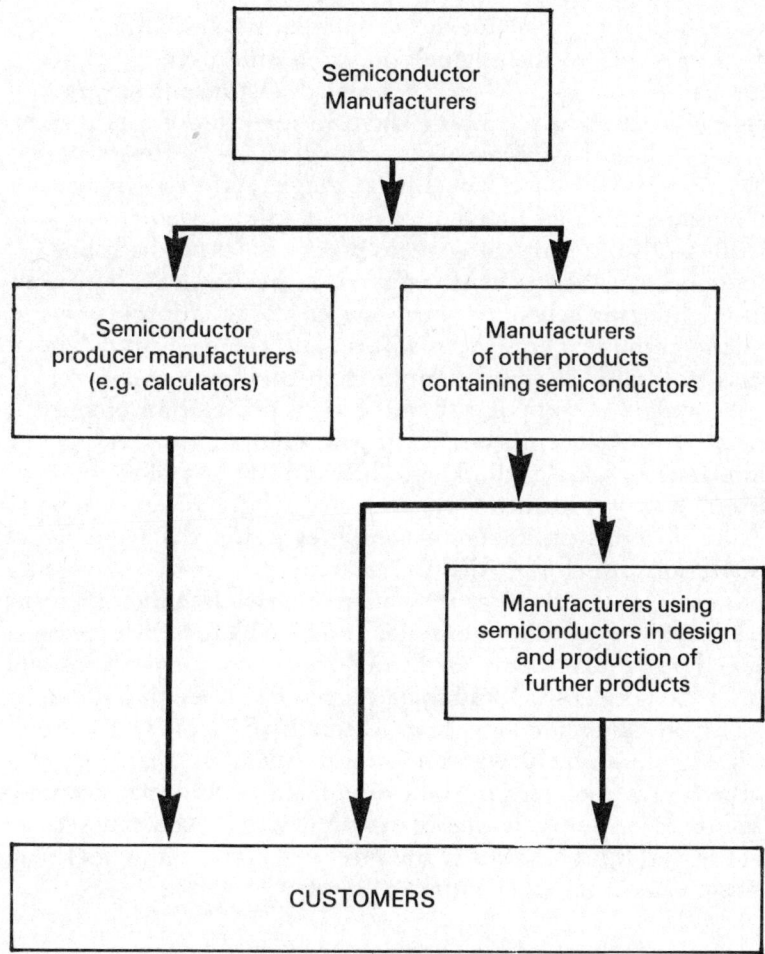

Figure 6.2 Semiconductor flow through industry

exacerbated as soon as at least one manufacturer in each sector designs 'electronic intelligence' into his products, because other manufacturers will almost certainly be forced to follow suit or cease to operate in that particular market. This process is expected to be underway by the early 1980s, across a broad range of appliance and consumer product markets.

This presents a challenge to companies employing design engineers and to the engineering profession itself. Experience has shown that even when a company's engineers are versed in electronic design, retraining them in microprocessors is often slow and laborious. Most engineers still regard 'software' design as more of an art, or 'black magic', than a science.[26] Nonetheless, a new breed of engineers will be needed, working with 'hardware' and 'software' as part of the same discipline.

At present, according to experts, it takes at least four years of engineering school to learn how to use microprocessor and microcomputer chips. This will remain the case until (and it may not happen) small computers in the home and at school have extended computer 'literacy'. It is difficult for engineers, who have not been brought up with computers, to adopt the appropriate ways of thinking. Software is a way of thinking in itself, and it will mean that engineers have to learn how to think in terms of making a computer perform a sequence of operations which they themselves write, rather than designing circuitry off-the-shelf, as they have very much tended to in the past. This represents the major threat which microprocessors pose for manufacturers, as the majority of companies are swept up in an accelerating and massive change in design philosophy based on a technology that is totally unfamiliar to them. Clearly, manufacturers cannot wait the four years or so it takes to train or retrain their design staffs, and many cannot afford to buy such scarce manpower in the open market, let alone wait for the results of the spread of home and schoolroom computers in general computer 'literacy'.

Consultants flourish

This explains why since the mid-1970s a thriving subindustry of independent consultants and microcomputer design and development companies, called 'systems houses', have sprung up in the USA and Europe. But, due to the same engineering bottlenecks which afflict their clients, consultants do not come cheap. It is quite common for consultants to charge a minimum of $5000 for product development. Users find that a gadget that costs only tens of dollars can lead to the expenditure of $5000 to $10000 to make it useful. The problem is that consultants do not drop in price like the semiconductor devices. However, without the help of a consultant, a lot of prospective users do not even know where to start. Part of the microprocessor puzzle is that there is so much hardware an offer in the marketplace. There were dozens of microprocessors, hundreds of memory chips and communication devices and nearly a hundred microcomputers by the end of 1978; and the list grows daily.

Programming problems

However, it is now common for semiconductor-makers to offer their clients a microcomputer development system. This kind of system makes it easier to program a microprocessor for specific tasks. However, by 1977, these systems often cost as much as $20000 a copy and could normally only be used with a single brand of microprocessor. This was seen as the germ of the type of tactic with which the big mainframe computer manufacturers had 'locked-in' their clients. It also reflected the fact that, despite their flexibility in theory, the current generation of microprocessors and microcomputer applications were 'dedicated' control systems on the whole. This led some maverick voices in the industry to suggest that the best way to design a microprocessor into a system was to treat it simply as another integrated circuit, which is precisely what Intel, in designing the microprocessor, had tried to avoid. But whatever the other uncertainties, it seems clear enough that, over the next five years at least, software consultants, systems houses and organisers of teach-ins and seminars will benefit from the shortage of skilled design engineers amongst equipment- and appliance-makers, and of programmers capable of working with machine codes.

This leads into the problem of a shortage of programmers. Like any other computer, a microprocessor is unable to think. The thinking has to be done by the programmer who relies on the microprocessor to carry out his instructions, precisely and very rapidly. But this represents a trap for the unwary, and not only for the engineers and managers brought up in robuster traditions where approximations seemed sufficient. The bulk of the world's programmers have been used to instruct large mainframe computers, which are easier to program than microcomputers, because they can be programmed in high-level languages such as Cobol and Fortran.[27]

At the basic level, as we have already seen, the primary roles of a microprocessor system are:

- Storing data;
- Retrieving all or any of the data, and performing simple functions on them and then, if required, either storing the results or delivering them as a coded putput.

The problem with the highly compact microsystem is that it has to be instructed in a low level language in 'real time'. For instance, if the input data are changing at a high speed, then the results of the processing will change at the same speed (for all practical purposes). At the same time, the processing functions are carried out at very high speeds anyway. If a microprocessor is incorporated in a control or feedback loop, it can respond almost instantaneously to any previously anticipated set of stimuli. Like any other computer, it is unable to cope with a situation unforeseen by the programmer; but with the microsystem this problem is in some respects exacerbated because of the speed at which the whole system operates.

Until very recently, the efficient programming of current microprocessors involved the use of machine codes. This is a primitive way of instructing a computer, rather like writing on stone tablets — everything has to be laboriously set out in digital language. Over the past fifteen or so years, machine code programming has been avoided, because of the use of compilers in large computers which have enabled programmers' throughput to be boosted by the use of high-level languages which resemble written English. See Appendix for fuller and more technical discussion of this issue.

Too few programmers

This is made worse by an overall shortage of programmers. It is estimated by one leading computer manufacturer, Digital Equipment, that the program capability of the world is only rising at an annual rate of 18 per cent, which is a slower growth rate than that of new installations of computers — mainframe, mini and micro.

However, it is argued that although severe, the problem of the shortage of programmers may be soluble. First, it is hoped that as computers are used more and more in schools and the home, computer 'literacy' will increase dramatically. So far, there is little evidence of this, mainly because computers in the school are still predominantly used for computer-aided instruction, however, Rockwell has had an encouraging experience training high-school children during vacations for routine DP tasks. This means that they are being used to teach children about non-computer, rather than computer subjects. Another argument put forward is that the growing disparity between hardware and software prices will render the concept of the stored program computer uneconomic and that the high cost of software can best be reduced by selling multiple copies. By 1978, for instance, Texas Instruments, recognising that the cost of customised software is too high, sought ways of making the software for small home computers mass-producible. One experiment was with the company's SR-59 programmable calculator. This is termed 'solid static software'. It works by plugging modules containing semiconductor memories into a calculator to turn it into a special purpose machine. In short, the customer programmer will gradually disappear, as the software industry moves from a service to a product orientation, selling its wares embedded in silicon.

Until this happens, as microprocessors and microcomputers become more powerful as well as cheaper, it will become economically attractive either to replace redundant processors with new ones with suitably modified instructions or to write inefficient programmes. This is especially feasible in an organisation which allows its programmers to work from home terminals, so that they can send programs into the office without worrying too much about syntax, have the programs 'cleaned' up on a word processor, and then feed the 'cleaned' up program into a minicomputer which can then translate the high-level language into the appropriate machine 'code'.

Not just electronics

If and when design and programming 'bottlenecks' have been cured, there will still be considerable demands on people and processes not directly involved with electronics. The quality and reliability of modern electronics is almost unbelievably high and the integrated circuit is an awesome technological innovation, just as the invention of the transistor had earlier been a most notable scientific breakthrough. Most circuits perform intricate functions with complete dependability at an extremely low cost. The limiting factor on performance, aside from the design and programming problems analysed earlier, is usually found in the peripherals. For instance, a pocket calculator is only as good as its battery, connections, keys and case and in the same way a digital watch is only as good as its display, its case, its battery and its interconnections. The semiconductor industry grew up with an extraordinary precision and attention to detail built into it right from the outset. This precision can be fairly readily extended to such high silicon-content products as calculators and wrist watches, but the problem becomes progressively more acute as the silicon content falls in proportion to the total product or system.

Other industries, brought up in robuster mechanical

traditions, find it difficult to match the perfections written into semiconductor electronics. This may cause greater difficulties than often envisaged when electronics begins to penetrate the domestic appliance market. It has already been a major feature in the automobile industry. As early as 1969 it had been hoped that by 1974, all of the USA's ten million new cars produced annually would contain up to twenty integrated circuits; but even by 1978 a market of that dimension had shown little sign of materialising. The motor manufacturers have argued that the conditions inside a car engine are hotter, noisier and dirtier than conditions experienced even in a missile. Moreover, while a component in a missile only has to function for a few minutes, a motor component must function for years at a fraction of the price of a missile component. Another problem has been the disparity in price and performance between microprocessors and the sensor equipment needed to feed information about the auto's performance to the processor integrated circuit. This is not all. The automobile manufacturers are concerned that the automobile must then be serviced and repaired by local mechanics, trained in the workings of the moving part engine and totally unfamiliar with solid state electronics.

These are good and sufficient reasons for the US automobile industry's resistance over an entire decade to the attractions of progressively cheaper powers of electronic logic. The auto industry has to live with its changes for a number of years, mainly because it has its capital invested in huge, mechanised production lines. This means that even minor changes are expensive and that it is scarcely feasible to indulge in experiments if the products are holding their position in the marketplace. This problem is exacerbated by the rapid changes in the semiconductor industry's products in terms of complexity and price. This contrasts markedly with the rhythmn of change in the auto industry where capital replacement costs are so high.

Similar problems occur in the telecommunications industry in countries like the USA and the UK, where telephone penetration has been high for many years. Existing telecommunications systems have massive capital sunk into them from the days when electromechanical exchanges were installed. The telephone authorities have to balance the cost of the service they can provide through the existing network with the cost of replacing the existing exchanges with purely electronic ones, and the swelling revenues which would result from the installation of a system which could expand subscriber services to such things as Viewdata and TASI. Like the auto industry, the telephone companies want to be pretty sure that when they decide to replace existing mechanical and electromechanical systems with electronic ones, the component technology is settled and not on the point of shifting to new levels of cheapness and reliability per 'logic-gate' or electronic function. This is why, with the progression from LSI to VLSI circuits over the next two or three years, many large equipment-makers and manufacturers may fear obscolescence in the basic electronic components less than they have during much of the 1970s.

Conclusions

We may recapitulate the practical problems facing business over the application of microelectronics as follows:

- The shortage of design engineers capable of designing electronic intelligence into products and the lack of programming capability to instruct the world's existing computer population and to pursue potential applications.
- A general unawareness that management needs to control a database and not a computer resource. The latter is fast becoming a widely 'distributed' system, extended down to peripherals, which renders the central computer and the DP department less and less important.
- The difficulties of meshing the precision of electronics with robuster and more approximate tractions, as the silicon-content in the end-product falls.

- The delicate balance between supplying the market from existing plant equipment and staff, which, as with the auto and telecommunications industries, may be very costly to replace or to use for experiments, and deciding when the competition using newer components and processes is getting too hot. In 1978, even AT&T ran a costly nationwide advertising campaign to hire sales and DP staff capable of providing the necessary back-up for a marketplace turning towards electronic products and systems.
- The difficulty of deciding when and if the basic electronic componentry has reached a plateau, so that a costly decision to change over from mechanical and/or electromechanical systems is taken at the optimum time from the standpoint of the reliability and cost of basic components.

The main likelihood is that once sector leaders, whether they be automobile manufacturers or domestic appliance makers, incorporate advanced control circuits into their products and processes, other manufacturers in the sector will have to follow suit. This will trigger an intensive struggle amongst the manufacturers for the limited supply of the appropriately skilled engineers, systems analysts, programmers and sales and maintenance teams. This will present a quite terrifying prospect for those companies that do not already have a design, DP, sales and service structure which can be switched over to the new products. By the early 1980s, the chances of building up an infrastructure from scratch will be extremely limited. This is why the impact of semiconductor electronics presents both a threat and a challenge.

Exxon vs IBM

A pointer to the growing infrastructure pressures occurred in early 1978 when Exxon Corp, which has around twenty information companies in the group, made a major move into the office equipment market. The company unveiled its Qyx electronic typewriter to compete head-on with IBM and Xerox. The Qyx was positioned to compete especially with the

IBM Selectric model. Independent observers saw considerable technical virtues in the Exxon machine. For one thing, it had been designed with only a handful of mechanical parts compared with hundreds in the Selectric. But it was soon realised that the biggest challenge facing Exxon was IBM's corps of 5000 highly trained salesmen, each making, at a conservative estimate, five calls a day. This example demonstrates the potential infrastructure problems facing companies, without Exxon's resources, trying to enter the marketplace with electronic products.

References

25. *The Microcomputers Marketplace in Western Europe, 1978-86,* Pactel.
26. Barker, H.A., *The Microprocessor in Control,* IEE.
27. Hilburn and Julich, *Microcomputers/Microprocessors:* Hardware, Software and Applications, Prentice-Hall, Inc.

Appendix 6.1: Micro talk

All computers — micro, mini or mainframe — need instructions. In theory, even the most basic computer, such as the Turing tape-marking machine imagined 40 years ago, can execute the most complicated procedures. Writing the necessary instructions (programs), however, can be exceedingly difficult and thus both costly and error-prone. The computer itself only recognises the pattern of 'bits', or binary digits, called machine code.

However with the development of digital computers, which incorporate such software organisers as compilers as well as large volumes of accessible memory, it has been possible to devise a hierarchy of languages as an aid to program writing. In higher-level languages (such as Fortran, Cobol or Pascal) entire routines consisting of tens or even hundreds of machine instructions are represented by a single statement. But a higher-level language is itself a program or set of programs which must be adapted to operate on a particular machine.

In many ways, software developments with microprocessors have paralleled those with early digital computers, with programs written initially in machine code, then in assembly language (which replaces binary notation with more concise and memorable symbols) and now, but still infrequently, in high-level languages.

Because the microprocessor has developed from components up rather than computers down, the penetration of software into microprocessor system design started at a low level and progress has remained slow. There have been serious physical obstacles in the way of advanced software too. For one thing, the cost of sufficient volumes of accessible memory have been too high, until recently, to design into microprocessor-driven systems for high-level language programming. For another, it has only just become possible to reach a high enough level of circuit complexity per chip to make the architecture of the processor chips more regular and at the same time versatile.

But now, with falls in memory costs and further increases in circuit density, there is a growing focus on software by microprocessor manufacturers in a drive to introduce higher-level languages that are easier and faster to use in writing programs. Three microprocessors announced in 1979 from Intel, Zilog and Motorola — the Intel 8086, the Z8000 and the MC 68000 — have a major share of their machine resources dedicated to improving their literacy in higher-level languages. This is made possible by their greater overall power. In terms of instructions and data capacity divided by speed of operation the Z8000, for instance is probably better than the Intel 8008 introduced in 1972, by a factor of more than 100.

The architecture of these fourth generation processors combines that all-important regularity with versatility. For instance, instead of the single accumulator design of the previous generation, the machines have several equivalent registers. Each can serve as an accumulator for arithmetic and logic operations and also hold a constant or point to an address in the memory. This means that an instruction that can be executed in one register can generally be executed in any of them. Moreover the machines carry a much greater volume of accessible memory than their predecessors at roughly a million bytes.

The savings from switching to higher-level languages are potentially enormous. Machine codes, which have to set out each step in the sequence in binary notation, are both cumbersome and time-consuming and therefore, by definition, costly. For example, a machine code completed by Teletronix Inc. for one of its graphic terminals involved a machine language program which ran to 65,000 characters, took over eight man-years to compile and cost around $300,000. A single line of higher-level language can do the job it takes approximately five lines of older language to accomplish, and the average programmer can only manage about 10 good lines of machine code a day.

Five years ago, software probably only accounted for 5% of the total cost of developing a microprocessor system. Now, it can top 70% of the total cost. This reflects soaring labour costs, exacerbated by programmer shortages, as well as the slow progress in writing machine language programs. Some experts claim that the use of higher-level languages can cut the cost of software by anything up to 75% and increase programming speeds by a factor of 10.

Another key advantage of a higher-level language program is what is known amongst DP people as 'portability': this is a program which can be switched, with a minimum of change, from one piece of hardware to another. In the past, microprocessor users have been 'locked in' by machine codes to particular models. Thus, despite the low hardware cost of processors, if a user wanted to change to another model it meant writing off much of his original software investment: often amounting to 10 to 15 man-years of software development.

But while the microelectronics industry assaults software costs, some computer scientists are pointing to a medley of deeper and probably less tractable problems. These problems are not intrinsically related either to the shortage of programmers — cited in the accompanying chapter — or to deficiencies in machine architecture, but to the software itself.

Although reductions in hardware cost and size, coupled with increases in operating speeds, have led to the prospect of a substantial increase in the magnitude of the problems which computer systems can theoretically tackle, a software 'threshold' may well have been crossed. This is the view, for instance, of the MIT's Joe Weizenbaum.

Up to fifteen years ago, a whole computer system was often devised and written by one person. But this was succeeded by team programming with decreasing emphasis, however, on the chief programmer team approach. Now, argues Weizenbaum, the job is done via a programming system rather than an organised team that is doing the work. A computer system, in other words, suffers the onslaught of many people. 'As a consequence', according to Weizenbaum, 'there are many systems for which there is no theory and no team of people who understand the whole thing.'

This is a large part of the reason why, with the move towards more pervasive and distributed data processing, another leading computer scientist, Edsgar Dijiskra, argues that, for software, the development of the microprocessor represents a major step backwards. Dijiskra is apt to address conferences on the virtual impossibility of proving the correctness even of a program which extends to only three lines.

For men like Weizenbaum and Dijiskra the impact of cheap electronic components on computing could be to harden the dangerous illusion that once a problem has apparently been solved by writing a program or hard wiring a machine then that problem has been solved for ever.

Arguably, this means that neither business in particular nor society in general should become too dependent on computer systems, given the little that is understood about such systems, their proneness to error, the problems of program maintenance, and the ways in which computers can often act on their instructions in unpredictable ways without in any way ceasing to be 'forthright.'

Nonetheless, despite the development of machines like the Z8000 and the Intel 8086, there is a natural and more mundane reason why the bulk of microelectronic components will probably be used primarily for electronic rather than computing tasks. This is that they will be used to replace existing mechanical and electro-mechanical control systems for the most part, which are not capable of executing complex functions and therefore their replacements will not call for extreme complexity or computing prowess.

7 Semiconductors: the world's toughest business

"in this industry we don't go in for bureaucratic rationalisations. We just fight like alley cats."

Robert Noyce

The world's programming capability and the availability of design engineers able to design 'electronic intelligence' into products will largely determine both the width of the application of advanced circuits (including microprocessor circuits) and the rate of the technology's diffusion beyond the computer, telecommunications and high silicon content industries. The main counterforce to this will be the drive amongst the semiconductor-makers (excluding IBM and AT&T which do not sell into the 'commercial' market) to sell their voluminous output.

Force-feeding the market

It is possible, and has already happened, that end-users will buy cheap and complex circuits — simply because they are so readily available and inexpensive — before they are ready to use them properly. This has happened up in the mainframe computer market, but for different reasons, where, as we have seen, the bulk of the 500000 or so computers which have been installed worldwide have either been underused or badly used. There could be a similar occurance in semiconductor applications.

Ironically, the semiconductor industry's sheer ability to reproduce increasingly complex circuits is also its Achilles Heel; the prospect that the semiconductor-makers may eventually produce far more powerful circuits than the market can absorb is very real. By 1985, according to one of the elders of the industry, it will be feasible to build a pocket calculator that will be more powerful and almost as fast as the world's most powerful computer (as at 1979), the $9 million Cray-I, built by Cray Research Inc. But this would be virtuosity for its own sake if the market could not use such a product. Hints of this prospective problem, as we have noted, have already occurred, for example, with the underuse of pocket calculators which include logarithmic functions, consumer resistance to 'digitalised' stereo equipment and the long resistance of Detroit to the incorporation of electronic devices in automobile engines.

Making the products usable

Another experienced head in the semiconductor industry warns that the industry's biggest problem is going to be to find ways of transforming all the innovation into viable products that are simple to use. This could well mean that the much vaunted VLSI circuits will only have limited uses over the next few years outside memory devices for the electronic data-processing industry.

So far, nearly 85 per cent of the industry's production (excluding the 1960s and early 1970s when the defence industries bought a lot of the industry's output) is ending up in the retail market in the form of TV games, digital timepieces and calculators. The industry, therefore, is increasingly concerned to encourage the automobile, telecommunications, domestic appliances, office equipment and industrial controls manufacturers to buy circuits. The need to do so is clear. It has been estimated that on present trends in capacity, the industry will only avoid permanent overcapacity if the equivalent of everybody in the world can be persuaded to possess a silicon version of a minicomputer by 1985. This is a stiff, if by no means impossible, goal.

A unique industry

One of the main problems in trying to analyse the impact of the semiconductor industry on the diffusion of semiconductor technology is that the industry itself, in terms of structure and personnel, is almost as bizarre (or advanced) according to the particular point of view, as its products. Its main characteristics are as follows:

- From nothing in 1960, sales of SICs (including microprocessors) are likely to reach $6 billion by 1980 and $11 billion by 1985. So it is a high growth industry.[28]
- But an exploding technology is coupled with persistent and often deep price cutting (even in times of under production); prices fall on average by 20 per cent a year. This makes it almost impossible to market the products.
- The industry has amoeba-like qualities: at least in the USA which still accounts for the bulk of it. This means that it does not combine very well. Its historic tendency has been to do the reverse — to split. This tends to make an already basically fiercely competitive industry even more competitive.
- The industry tends, therefore, to avoid mergers when revenues are pinched (which they are periodically) and to try instead to protect revenues by 'vertical integration' by means of 'component-up' moves into end-user markets, like calculators and watches and now computers: but this could lead in the end to collisions with the very end-users which the industry at present needs to supply with components, and has already led to severe trading losses for some semiconductor majors.

- All this is exacerbated by the determined effort by the Japanese electronics industry to 'bootstrap' itself into the advanced circuit industry to compete with the Americans in the world SIC market by the early 1980s, as an essential step in the Japanese 'game-plan' of competing across the board in sophisticated electronic goods — including computers — by the mid-1980s.
- The industry tends to be run by brilliant electronics engineers and solid state physicists rather than by marketing or financial men. These engineers, who are often daring entrepreneurs, do not always understand or foresee the reluctance of potential end-users to change their production lines and their service networks to incorporate electronic 'intelligence' in the place of conventional mechanical and electromechanical systems. The prime, and often repeated, example of this resistance has been the Detroit motor industry.
- The industry's tradition, during its short history, has been for frequent and informal contacts, by word of mouth, between design engineers in competing firms and for top engineers to be permanently and potentially 'on the hoof'. This often makes patents almost academic. It also increases the pressures on firms to establish 'beachheads' in the market, often by loss-leading, by being first with particular products.

Quoting below costs

Not surprisingly, executives in semiconductor firms often claim that theirs is the most difficult business in the world. One of the original industry leaders said that in over twenty years in the industry, he can hardly remember a successful price increase. Also, six-month forward prices are often quoted at below current costs. Another executive points to the odd fact, which violates all commercial logic, that in advanced electronics the cheapest product is often the best. Both features are due to the operation of the famous 'learning curve'.

A little history

But before turning to the 'learning curve' and to the current and potential pressures on the industry, a brief history of the semiconductor business is in order.[29] This immediately highlights the US industry's strange paradox; that for all its fierce competition, it is a strangely family affair. The real founder of the industry was William Shockley, co-inventor of the transistor and winner of a Nobel Prize. Shockley Transistor was founded in 1956 at Palo Alto with the intention of developing transistors for the defence industries which would be able to function in high temperatures. But only a year later, eight of Shockley's ablest collaborators left, and with the backing of Fairchild Camera and Instrument Corp set up Fairchild Semiconductor. The new firm prospered, by, amongst other things, developing the planar production process. But it too eventually began to spawn its engineers who formed businesses on their own account, on the basis of venture capital.

As a result, Santa Clara County, California, usually nicknamed Silicon Valley, is speckled with more than forty firms that were founded by the so-called 'Fairchildren', men who originally worked as technicians at Fairchild Semiconductor. The most remarkable firm spawned by Fairchild is Intel Corp, founded in 1968 by Robert Noyce and Gordon Moore, both from Fairchild. As we have already seen, in Chapter 1, Intel engineers developed the microprocessor which was the key breakthrough in LSI technology. Intel's shipments now account for some 25 per cent of the world market in advanced SICs.

Much of the atmosphere of the industry is reflected in the remarkable career of Lester Hogan. When at Motorola, Hogan had attracted no less than eighteen semiconductor engineers from General Electric. Then, when he moved from Motorola to Fairchild, Hogan took with him the entire senior management of Motorola's semiconductor division. Moreover, when Fairchild lured Hogan from Motorola, they offered him a salary of over $100000, an interest-free loan of $5.4 million and stock options on 100000 shares in the company, on which, within a year, Hogan was reckoned to have made a paper profit of some $2.5 million. Since the Hogan deal in 1968, the industry has tended to measure deals offered to its top men in 'units of Hogan'. There are few industries where this would have happened, or where the matter would have been treated with such subsequent sang-froid.

There have been a number of studies trying to determine how and why Silicon Valley became the centre of the SIC industry, despite the fact that Texas Instruments and Motorola, both billion dollar SIC makers, are located elsewhere: in Dallas and Phoenix respectively. It has been suggested, for instance, that the Universities of Stanford and Berkeley were important ingredients in this, but there is no firm evidence to support this, as the industry is largely 'technology-driven' rather than 'science-based'. The simplest explanation is that Silicon Valley was where Shockley had decided to set up his pioneer firm when he moved from the Eastern Seaboard. The area was pleasant, and had a sufficiently high standard of living, to encourage the subsequent amoebic splits to take place in the same vicinity.

Probably the strongest reason why the industry has remained so concentrated in Silicon Valley is that the industry leaders accept that 'cross-fertilisation' and employee mobility is almost certainly a net benefit to a high technology business where people with similar intellectual backgrounds and interests need to compare notes easily and informally. It is noticeable how little of the industry's research is reported in learned papers, read to seminars, or published in university proceedings. There is little premium, as we have noted, on basic research. The RGD people in the industry openly admit that they have little understanding of the basic physics of complex circuits, although physicists at IBM are almost certainly doing basic research work on this. But in the commercial SIC industry, it is often difficult for a researcher to find a spare production line where he can experiment with ideas and designs, such is the pressure to reproduce existing engineering designs in maximum volume until that product is threatened. The more so, as around a quarter of all the circuits produced, are not deemed fit for consumption.

Thus, it is no surprise to find that as a proportion of sales, basic research in semiconductors had dropped from nearly 30 per cent in the late 1950s to probably less than 5 per cent today. Furthermore, about 80 per cent of the industry's basic research is carried out by IBM and AT&T which do not sell in the commercial market. It is significant in this respect that Texas Instruments talks these days of 'total technical effort' which includes some aspects of marketing.

Shifting from science to technology

The major business development of the industry, apart from the spread of the 'Fairchildren' into a host of new high-technology companies, was the industry's shift from dependence on military and aerospace orders into mass consumer or retail markets during the 1970s. Although early in 1979, several semiconductor companies, led by Texas Instruments and Rockwell, backed a $150 million Pentagon project to develop superfast VLSI circuits and tightly-packed memory devices.

In the 1950s, because of the scientific orientation of the transistor industry, which had grown out of basic research in the late 1940s, the semiconductor industry was largely seen a triumph of science and vast sums were spent by larger firms on research laboratories to push the scientific discoveries further. For a time, this was the main impetus of the industry. This fitted in with the needs of the defence and space industries which had demanded high performance and reliability, whatever the cost, and which had (and still do, for the most part) insisted on manual rather than automatic testing.

However by the late 1950s and early 1960s, some in the industry, led by men like Robert Noyce, began to realise that the industry's progress would depend more on the efficiency of its technology rather than its scientific research. As we saw in Chapter 1, much of the impetus behind the transformation of the discrete transistor into microminiaturised transistors layered into blocs in integrated circuits had been technological. As one industry leader put it, there began to be an awareness around 1960 that solid state physics had left the laboratory for the factory. So, whereas in the 1950s and early 1960s the defence industries had funded important developments in semiconductor technology and taken much of the industry's output, such firms as Fairchild based their success on selling to other customers, and on trying to consolidate the existing technology into viable products rather than on trying to meet the exact requirements of the 'custom' built military market.

The force of the learning curve

The whole of manufacturing industry uses the concept of the 'learning curve', but nowhere more pointedly than in the semiconductor industry. The concept depicts the relationship between the volume of production and unit costs, by which unit cost declines as production volume grows. Texas Instruments, for instance, has found that every time output doubles, the price per unit drops to 73 per cent of its previous level. This means that market share becomes the primary aim. Being first, or as near as makes no odds, into a product, and then getting away as big a sales volume as possible, while sometimes loss-leading to establish a 'beachhead' is the tactic; while all the time learning how to lower production costs. All this happens in a climate where prices are tending to fall anyway, and it strikes especially savagely when the industry suffers a cyclical downturn. For instance, in 1970, a tussle between Texas Instruments and Fairchild led to a price fall in one component from 75 to 9 cents in only eighteen months.

The 'learning curve' has tended to divide the industry into those companies which operate at the front-end of the process and those that operate lower down the curve. Intel and Zilog are prime examples of companies that concentrate on innovation and on being first on the market with industry 'standards'. The innovative companies are comparatively low volume, high profit margin, operations. At the other end of the spectrum is Texas Instruments, which often comes in as the cycle matures. The tactic at this stage is to dramatically lower product prices to shake out as much of the competition as possible and then rely on improvements in production techniques to get away a high volume of sales on very low unit profit margins. Nevertheless, the distinctions between the Intels and Texas Instruments may now be close to disappearing. Intel's co-founder, Gordon Moore, has developed a series of graphs showing the growth of circuit complexity against time. Following the incredibly fast rate of innovation in this respect between 1971 and 1978, Moore has begun to query whether, at much above current levels of complexity, it is possible to identify the products which can command the volume market necessary to make them viable.

The force of the 'learning curve' is the basic ingredient in the price fall per electronic function from nearly $10 in 1960 to less than 1 cent today. It also lies behind the fall in the price of an electronic calculator from $100 in 1970 to under $10 today. It leads to the kind of distortion which enables one industry leader to comment that 'in this industry cheapest is usually best' and another to claim that it is the toughest business in the world. It is also, by definition, the force behind the irresistable attraction of circuit components in terms of availability and cost. Some estimates suggest that the effect of the semiconductor 'learning curve' will be to power the electronics industry, as a whole, from its current annual shipments of just over $100 billion to over $300 billion by the late 1980s. This would make the industry the world's fifth largest, behind oil, autos, steel and chemicals — each with sales of around $500 billion — but each pervaded by electronic componentry. It is here that the Japanese come in, as we saw in Chapter 1.

Japan Inc. runs it hard

By 1976 the Japanese were already playing the game hard, to establish a 'beachhead' in advanced electronics. In 1977, Japanese companies managed to snatch 25 per cent of the US market in microelectronic memories for computers: the 4K and 16K random access memory devices. What appalled the US producers was not the price of the Japanese chips, but their low failure rate. The Japanese were testing the chips on the assembly line in a way which would leave a purely commercial semiconductor operation 'swimming in red ink'. A top planner at Texas Instruments in Dallas, the biggest microelectronics company in the world (apart from IBM, which doesn't however sell into the commercial market), explained that 'the Japanese are a tremendous threat because they can run that "learning curve" against a national P&L account'. This is true. Japanese business tends to run on much lower margins than business in the USA and the UK, because the emphasis is on sales volume, and the business is not judged on a series of annual accounting periods.

However not everything went right for the Japanese. The rise of the yen not only pushed up the dollar cost of Japanese labour, but blunted the competitive edge of a lot of Japanese products. This was especially so with computers. Although the Americans started to fret, estimates from within Japan itself indicated that in 1977/8 the Japanese computer industry would export less than 5 per cent of its output in the year to April.

Something of an embarrassment occurred in the summer of 1977 when the Japanese computer company, Fujitsu, became the first company in the world to produce sample batches of a 64K ram device. These devices had been singled out by the industry as being important examples of the new technology of very large-scale integration. There was an intense race between the US majors and the Japanese to produce the first devices for the market. The feeling was that whoever did so would win an important psychological advantage and give himself an important 'beachhead' in the market. It looked as though the Japanese had succeeded, with the Fujitsu chip, but it turned out to be 'technologically primitive', being little more than four 16K rams wired together, with resulting interconnection and power supply problems. The scare was over — temporarily.

However, delay in Japanese computer exports and the Fujitsu affair provided no basis for complacency in Western business circles. It was widely accepted by 1978 that the industrialised country which can design the new electronics into the widest range of goods, and which can then produce those goods with the aid of computers and electronic controls, will win the battle in the world marketplace.

As we have seen, Japan is regarded by many observers as the country most likely to force the pace in the market by being the first major producer to embrace the new 'heartland' electronic technology. The danger for the USA and Europe is that their business systems are less integrated and less likely than their Japanese competitiors, therefore, to work with the semiconductor makers to get the best out of the technology. Indeed, the US semiconductor industry resembles an enclave in the US business scene, rather than an integral part of it.

However, the probable success of the Japanese in the world semiconductor market by the early 1980s would invalidate two arguments put forward to explain the US domination of the field during the 1960s and 1970s:

- That a highstream technology like microelectronics requires the support of large military and aerospace industries.
- That the development of a standard electronic component, as opposed to 'custom-built' components, requires a continental-sized market.

The Japanese experience seems to belie both these explanations, although the US industry greatly benefited form the support of the military during the costly early phase in the twenty-year semiconductor 'learning curve'. This is why the development of the Japanese advanced integrated circuit industry between 1976-8 was being operated against a 'national P&L account'.

At the same time, the progressively successful Japanese semiconductor drive points to the enigmatic qualities of Japanese business organisation to most Americans. Ever since the US semiconductor industry became largely independent of the military and aerospace industries, it has been left to its own devices. Many industry leaders suggest that the intense competitiveness of the industry, which has led to many casualties, is the main reason for its success in terms of products and prices. In short, throughout the 1970s the US industry has taken a 'market-led', technological route; or, more precisely, in the words of Intel's Robert Noyce, it has set out 'to engineer good products and then sell them again and again.'

Why Europe lags

The structure of the US industry contrasts markedly with the European electronics scene. The main differences are as follows:

- Unlike the USA, European countries have seen their electronics industries rationalised. Both the French and the British governments, for instance, saw fit to amalgamate existing companies into giant national ventures, such as GEC-English Electric and Sescosem, with which to answer the US challenge.
- This has meant that few semiconductor experts have broken away from established European companies to start their own firms, or to join new ventures. This has partly reflected the lack of venture capital in Europe, and partly the reluctance of most European companies to recruit from their competitors.
- A partial effect of this has been for some of Europe's brightest electronics technicians to emigrate to the USA, where they

have been attracted by the superior opportunities, high salaries and stock options offered by US semiconductor companies. Examples are Fairchild's Wilfred Corrigan and Motorola's Colin Crook (although Crook returned to the UK in 1978).

Very largely for these reasons, Europe has tended to leave the market in standard electronic parts to the Americans and has concentrated on the market in 'custom-built' circuits on a national scale: a policy successfully pursued, for instance, by Britain's Ferranti. But by 1978, the Europeans suddenly realised that they were going to be entirely dependent on either US or Japanese parts by the early 1980s for mass-market applications, just as electronic componentry moved into its pervasive phase. Some European equipment-makers searched for US partners with whom to arrange joint-product deals. Britain's GEC, for instance, secured an arrangement with Fairchild and France's Thomsen-CSF with Motorola. But at the same time, US majors, such as Texas Instruments and Motorola, were supplying European markets from UK plants.

Korea bids for customers and supremacy

But is it not simply that the Europeans are in search of short cuts to standard component technology and production techniques via the Americans. Some of the American semiconductor majors themselves have been in need of external finance and resources to expand their capacity both for the US domestic market and the EEC markets. It is estimated that the US industry now needs to invest at least $1 billion a year to be in a position to supply the likely bulge in domestic demand for circuits in the early 1980s, but at the same time it is widely assumed that each investment dollar in the industry yields extra sales of only $2. This has put considerable pressure on some semiconductor companies which have been forced by the persistent fall in product prices and the force of the learning curve to concentrate on sales volume rather than profit margins.

A possible solution has been for American companies to expand outside the US on the back of foreign finance, often direct or indirect government finance. A case in point is Mostek which has embarked on a $74 million, three-phased, project, to operate from Ireland, using mostly Dublin government funds.

Other American companies, with total overheads (especially labour costs) in mind, have been focussing on the Far East. It is in this context that South Korea has embarked on perhaps the most sophisticated electronics strategy in the world. The Seoul government is to pump $600 million (which, pro rata, is ten times more than the UK government, for instance, is spending to support UK-based microelectronics) in an effort to create the world's most advanced zone for semiconductor production. The plan is to turn the Gumi industrial estate, south of Seoul, into a superior Far Eastern version of California's Silicon Valley.

By 1982, it is planned to have at least 12 semiconductor factories in operation at Gumi, mostly run by joint Korean-American ventures under 40/60 equity arrangements, with the Koreans holding the majority stake. But according to Glen Madland, vice-president of Integrated Circuit Engineering, the American consultancy advising the Koreans, Gumi will offer anyone who goes to Korea the best available infrastructure in the world in terms of site, plant, availability of LSI technology, pure gases and technical personnel.

The Koreans have created a university campus at Gumi, which under the plan will produce 600 electronics engineers and technicians a year. Meanwhile, a corps of personnel is available apprenticed at leading American firms such as Fairchild. The Korean aim is not only to reduce to virtually zero their current ratio of electronic imports to electronic exports of over 70 per cent, but also (and in order to achieve this) to outgun other Far Eastern centers such as Taiwan, Singapore and Hong Kong as well as Europe for American custom in joint ventures, and overtake Japanese industry by 1990 in world electronics markets.

Table 7.1 American league

Sales of integrated circuits

	$m 1978	% increase since 1973
Texas Instruments	669	84
National	338	166
Motorola	329	137
Intel	300	417
Fairchild	255	37
AMD	132	529
Mostek	120	208

Fairchild Microcosm of an industry

However, probably the most poignant illustration of the complex of pressures on the independent semiconductor manufacturers is the recent history of Fairchild Camera and Instrument, the company which started the modern semiconductor industry in 1957 when it hired eight scientists who had all previously worked at Shockley Semiconductor Laboratories to attempt further exploitation of the then relatively new diffusion and oxide masking techniques. But by 1979, having spawned the famous 'Fairchildren' mentioned earlier, Fairchild was number five in the US industry behind Texas Instruments, National Semiconductor, Motorola and Intel in terms of sales of integrated circuits. Moreover, by common consent, it was behind the leaders in cheap microprocessors and MOS memory circuits, even if it still led in high-speed logic devices for computers. Its financial profile left something to be desired too. Despite a sharp recovery of $24.8 million in 1978 earnings to $534 million, Fairchild only returned 13 per cent on its equity compared to an industry average of 18.6 per cent.

It was almost inevitable that with its erratic and often

disappointing performance but its critical mass of nearly $400 million in annual semi-conductor sales, Fairchild would become the target of bids. The original favourite to go for the company was Britain's GEC with whom Fairchild had signed a $40 million joint-product agreement in late 1978 to make and market standard products based on MOS, CCD and LSI technology in the UK to supply the markets of Western Europe.

But there were hints that GEC needed Fairchild less than Fairchild needed GEC. The head of GEC Electronic Devices, Howard Losty, commented that the tie-up with Fairchild completed GEC semiconductor's strategy 'by enabling GEC to change from a 'custom-house' to a volume supplier of standard circuits'. For Fairchild, according to David Marriott, managing director of GEC/Fairchild in the UK, GEC with net cash reserves in excess of $400 million and itself a major consumer of semiconductors seemed to present almost a mirror image of the tried and failed policy in Fairchild's case of moving component up into consumer products such as video games, digital watches and calculators in the mid-1970s in an attempt to buoy up and improve profit margins. As Marriott put it 'LSI business is highly capital intensive and costly, almost too much for a single corporation to handle on its own these days. Here we have two major corporations sharing the burden.'

However by the Spring of 1979, despite a month of intense trading on Wall Street in Fairchild shares on the prospect of a GEC bid, it was Gould Inc. which made a move with a cash and preferred stock bid of $54 per Fairchild share. But Fairchild saw the bid as a hostile bid and forced Gould to up the ante first to $57 a share and then $70 a share for half the Fairchild stock. Most analysts reckoned that Gould, a highly successful electrical equipment company, but with a highly regimented corporate management structure and with 70 per cent of its sales in products incorporating semiconductor devices, would try to shake up the Fairchild management. In California, there was talk of a mass exodus from Fairchild should Gould try to impose a policy of centralised management by objectives on the semiconductor company.

Then the Gould bid was superceded in late May by a $66 per share all-cash bid from the French oil services and precision equipment conglomerate, based in New York, Schlumberger. The difference between Gould and Schlumberger was that the Schlumberger chief executive, Jean Riboud, quickly made it clear that in any merger with his group Fairchild would operate as a separate subsidiary with its present management. Not surprisingly the Fairchild board unanimously supported the Schlumberger counter to Gould's bid.

The bidding for Fairchild demonstrated three things: that American end-users were becoming increasingly anxious to secure their supplies of integrated circuits: that Fairchild needed access to substantial cash backing and that an alternative to 'vertically integrating' component up into end products was for a semiconductor company to become a part of an end-user's 'backward integration' into component supplies, so long as the end-user had a voluminous cash-flow.

Designer interaction

A key part of the logic behind the drive by European and Far Eastern equipment makers to tie-up joint-product agreements with US semiconductor companies and the competitive bidding for Fairchild by two American end-users is the need for what is termed 'designer interaction.' According to Dr Ian Macintosh of Macintosh Consultants a standard electronic circuit for industry emerges from a close liaison between the circuit designer in the semiconductor company and the system designer, at the equipment maker. The argument is that when the semiconductor product eventually emerges as an industry standard, but is initially in short supply, the first end-user to benefit, and thereby gain in a competitive advantage in his sector, will be the one who has been involved in this interactive process.

Macintosh argues that European industry, partly because it had not had anything more than a 'custom'-chip industry, lags at least two years behind the US and Japan in this respect. It flows from this that for a country to be internationally competitive in products with a comparatively high silicon content, or where electronic controls are otherwise important, there must be an intimate relationship between circuit designers and systems designers in manufacturing industry.

However, the widespread development of 'designer interaction' depends on an automatic technology transfer between the world's leading circuit builders and designers on the one hand and equipment makers wherever they may be based on the other. This is the main purpose behind GEC's broad agreement with Fairchild and also behind the Korean's $600 million project at Gumi. It is also the purpose behind Britain's famous Inmos project.

The strange case of Inmos

But, perhaps, the most startling move in the industry was made by a British Labour government in July 1978 when it announced that it was putting $100 million towards a 'greenfield' semiconductor company which would aim to make 'standard' parts for the world market by the early 1980s.[30] A key adviser on the feasibility study had been Dr Ian Macintosh. The UK initiative, called Inmos, is worth documenting in detail not only because it was the first new semiconductor venture starting from scratch since 1975, but because it highlights some of the main features of the semiconductor venture starting from scratch since 1975, but because it highlights some of the main features of the semiconductor business: its incestuousness, its competitiveness and its uncertainty. What makes it especially bizarre is the fact that it is to be funded by the UK National Enterprise Board (which was at least conceived as an instrument of socialist intervention), and yet if it is successful it will make its founders millionaires. What is more, two out of the three founder members are Americans.

The Inmos boss is Dr Richard Petritz, a Texan venture capitalist, who had once headed up R&D at Texas Instruments and been a founder member of both Fairchild and Mostek. His founder colleagues were Dr Paul Schroeder, a one-time top memory circuit designer for Mostek and Dr Iann Barron a leading British computer expert, concerned with the Inmos strategy.

No sooner had the establishment of Inmos been formally announced in July 1978 when Mostek issued a writ against Inmos. This was typical of the industry. A preliminary injunction filed in a Dallas court on 22 September 1978 sought to prohibit five former Mostek employees — including Dr Schroeder — from revealing confidential information gained at Mostek to the new company. If successful, the action would have stopped the Inmos men from working. The injunction also asked that Inmos be barred from hiring any more Mostek engineers. The injunction failed when the Texas District Judge expressed the view that 'Mostek had failed to show that either its techniques or information have been or will be utilised or disclosed'. The industry has found that legal action rarely works. For instance, an injunction failed to stop Lester Hogan from taking the entire senior management of Motorola's semiconductor division with him to Fairchild. However, actions to stop further poaching have sometimes been successful. For instance in 1969, IBM managed to stop Cogar Corporation from recruiting IBM personnel, but not until Cogar had poached seventy employees.

Nonetheless, there was a further twist to the Mostek/Inmos wrangle, when three of the five defendants in the Dallas case resigned from Inmos, after less than two months with the company, to set up an independent consultancy. The consultancy started with one client, none other than Mostek. An added irony of the suit was that Petritz of Inmos had been one of the founders of Mostek and a golfing companion of the Mostek president, M.J. Sevin. There was no evidence that Sevin took any personal relish in the action against Inmos. But, as we have seen, the commercial logic of the US semiconductor industry allows no room for sentimentality. Sevin himself said at the time of the Inmos suit 'it's war. The semiconductor companies are out to destroy one another.' The main thing

Sevin had to do was to show his shareholders that he had done everything in his power to stop Inmos dead. This was the more urgent because of the threat from Japan. The semiconductor industry was cut-throat enough without either the Japanese or a 'greenfield' venture like Inmos entering the market. In short, the semiconductor companies are playing a 'zero-sum' game with one another: one company's success is usually another's failure.

The Mostek/Inmos suit had all the ingredients of the personnel problems in an industry where the top people all know each other: companies poaching from each other, then taking the case abortively to court, all manner of elaborate measures to outgun the opponent. But perhaps the main dimension of the case surrounded the person of Schroeder. This is because, as we have already seen in describing the operation of the 'learning curve', the company which can bring out the latest generation of microprocessor or memory to find general acceptance — that is, which becomes the industry 'standard' — will make massive profits on that product, forcing the competitors to buy a licence in the circuit's technology simply to stay in the race. This puts enormous pressure on the top design engineers to come up with the products quickly enough and efficiently enough to corner the market. It also puts great pressure on the semiconductor companies to keep other companies from poaching their top design engineers: hence the action taken by Sevin to get Schroeder back. Hence the Lester Hogan saga. Schroeder had been crucial to Mostek in the design of 4K and 16K memory devices, which had given Mostek some 20 per cent of the market in memory circuits.

Despite the success of Inmos in attracting and keeping Schroeder and building a high-flying design team around him, what chance has it of surviving in an already oversupplied industry, where each product market is dominated by one or two companies only with almost everyone else out of the race? It is not the purpose of this book to judge the commercial viability of Inmos, but to set out the way in which its basic strategy — which is unique in view of the fact that Inmos is the first start-up operation in the industry since Zilog in 1974 —

highlights the main issues confronting the industry as it moves into the 1980s.

By necessity, the Inmos strategy is based on a heavy degree of 'contrathink' about 'usable' technology, the extent to which semiconductor makers should stray into end-user markets, and the optimum corporate structure in an industry where the parameters are again on the point of change. The 'usable' technology: while Texas Instruments talks about 256K memory circuits by 1985 and 10 million functional units per circuit by 1990, Inmos intends to buck the trend. Dr Barron incorporated his view and much else besides in a report he co-authored for the British Department of Industry's Computer, Systems, and Electronics Requirement Board (CERB) before he joined Petritz at Inmos. One of the main points in the report was that electronic controls will for the most part replace mechanical or electromechanical controls, which are not capable of executing complex control functions; therefore, their replacements will not require extreme complexity.

The Barron philosophy

Barron, as the Inmos strategist, sees the development of the 64K RAM circuit level of complexity as the key development. This does not mean the now famous 64K memory device over which there was such a fierce psychological war between the Americans and the Japanese in 1978, but the 64K RAM programmable chip as a 'standard' device. This is what Barron and the Inmos team think will satisfy the requirements of the mass-market at least until the mid-1980s.

Barron has long held the view that each silicon chip should have as much memory and processing power as possible etched on to it as the circuit density moves from LSI to VLSI levels of complexity. Moreover, Barron believes that beyond a 64K RAM level of complexity, there may well be all kinds of possibly costly blocks to development, such as diffraction problems and circuit leakages. Barron argues that the whole problem with semiconductors is yield in a production situation. Whereas it is easy to make things work in a laboratory, it is much more difficult to investigate the process within a production-type environment. Unlike Texas Instruments, Barron suggests that beyond the lower range of VLSI circuit density, the costs per circuit may start to rise again. It is therefore likely that the core Inmos product by 1982 will be a 64K RAM programmable silicon chip with between 4K and 16K of memory etched onto it, thereby giving it ample room for processing power.

This is why Petritz takes Intel as the Inmos yardstick. Intel had been formed from scratch in 1967 by Robert Noyce and Gordon Moore from Fairchild, and by 1971 it had made a key breakthrough in the then new LSI technology by designing and making the first microprocessor. The Inmos strategy is to do with VLSI technology what Intel did with LSI technology. The founder members are confident that $100 million is enough to accomplish this objective, and point to the profitability of Intel which has never been one of the industry's large turnover companies. But they concede that the cost of starting a semiconductor company has reached such a level that it is only a viable proposition now for one or two large multinationals or a national government.

Barron suggests that the 64K RAM programmable device will cater for most market needs. The CERB report hinted at the reasons for this assumption. The report saw information and data processing as being more like an extension of the electricity supply than the telephone system: almost something that will, like other electrical utilities, be powered from three-pin sockets. This in turn is close to the assumption of the major US computer manufacturer, mentioned in Chapter 3, that the computer will become an underused utility as the 1980s unfold. The key aspect of the proposed Inmos device is that it should be as variable in its end-use as possible. That is, it should be usable as a central component in a small computer, a learning aid, an intelligent telephone or a Viewdata/Teletext system.

This leads to another part of the Inmos 'contrathink'. The

Inmos strategy is to sell components, not systems or final products. But the US majors like Fairchild, National Semiconductor and Texas Instruments have gone 'component-up' into such end-user markets as calculators, digital watches, video games and computers. But in 1977, many of the semiconductor companies in these markets ended up with trading losses, as we saw earlier in the study of Fairchild.

The argument for moving into end-user markets is now familiar. It is a way of 'spreading the overhead' and getting into higher value-added activities than circuits on their own, where prices are falling by at least 30 per cent a year on average. A prime example of the industry's move into end-user markets has been National Semiconductor, which had sales of nearly $500 million by 1977. The company's decision to move into computer manufacture was twofold: first, as circuits become more integrated and prices fall further, the manufacturer is faced with the prospect of declining revenues unless he does some basic restructuring to get into the business of systems and end-products. The second main consideration is that, some day, computers will just be tin boxes mostly full of air, with just a few integrated circuits in them. Thus, National had already withdrawn from calculator manufacture by 1978 and also focused its digital watch production on the more upmarket timepieces. The reason for this was that the company saw that the markets in both these products, which have high proportions of silicon, were dictated by the same forces which operate in the circuit market itself. The same does not apply as the new generation of computers built solely on the basis of LSI circuits comes onto the market. Those components will themselves be so complex that the manufacturers will have to build up a substantial capability in programming just to produce them. In addition, the new powerful microcomputers will need to be backed by software developed by the manufacturers if they are to have any charisma in the marketplace. This is the forward momentum in some parts of the semiconductor industry that is carrying the component manufacturers into computer programming and the marketing of complete ranges of machines. Looked at the other way round, Intel's Robert Noyce has suggested, half seriously, that mainframe computer makers like Burroughs could probably be just as well off buying all its hardware from National Semiconductor.

This is a logic which Barron at Inmos accepts, but he sees a considerable danger in ending up on a collision course with giants like IBM and Digital Equipment, Fujitsu and Hitachi in Japan and ICL in the UK. By 1979 IBM, for instance, seemed to be jolting the 'plug-compatible' manufacturers who had been slicing into the mainframe market since 1976. The Inmos approach is to supply the equipment-makers with circuits — but circuits which Inmos understand as 'systems' — rather than compete with them in their own markets. For one thing, the success of companies like IBM is less to do with the equipment they make than with the huge sales teams and the after-sales service, which only very large electronics companies can support.

Parameter companies

This leaves the final main plank of the Inmos strategy. The rudiments of the Petritz/Barron approach to corporate structure is dramatic. petritz takes a leaf out of the book of the historian of science Dr Thomas Kuhn, *The Structure of Scientific Revolutions,* by arguing that technology moves in 'leaps', and that when this happens the parameters change. In electronics, the recent 'leaps' have been from MSI to LSI and by 1979-80 to VLSI. Petritz argues that as the technology 'leaps' it renders obsolete both a lot of the people and the capital equipment involved with the technology being replaced. On this argument, it can be better to start as nearly as possible from scratch, with 'unencumbered' people and system-built plant and equipment than to try and adapt an existing team and plant to the new technology. Clearly, this is an unobtainable ideal, but Petritz and Barron, again pointing to the example of Intel in the late 1960s, think that a 'greenfield' operation has a better chance of making the transition than companies formed under the old technology. The Inmos team, and indeed many in the US semiconductor industry, point to the fact that large companies like GE and RCA failed to make the grade as independents in the circuit market, because they were not flexible enough, or able, as Charles Sporck, president of National Semiconductor likes to put it 'to turn round on a dime'.

Conclusions

Whether Inmos succeeds or not is no immediate concern of this study. But its very formation and its guiding concepts are important. They provide a microcosm of the whole semiconductor industry, which is poised to move into yet another area of technology — the VLSI circuit. The industry is faced with basic decisions about the market's requirements in terms of complexity of circuits and its own long-run economies. Does it move component-up into end-user markets? What kind of customer services in terms of software and applications does it need to provide? As the industry starts to sell components, which are themselves systems, how does it relate to the equipment-makers? Does it compete with them direct? It is quite clear that not only is Inmos a microcosm of the whole semiconductor industry but that the semiconductor industry itself is a microcosm of the bulk of industry and commerce, looking ahead to the mid-1980s. The world's leading semiconductor makers have found that the complexity of their products has started to catapult them into new areas of business, which demand more research, different management approaches and, above all, clinical definitions, and in some cases, redefinitions of their basic strategy. By definition, as electronics moves into its 'pervasive phase', the upheaval facing the semiconductor industry will soon be followed by a similar upheaval in a wide range of user industries: from automobiles and telecommunications to domestic appliances and office equipment.

Much of the debate about the foregoing was covered in a public debate between none other than Lester Hogan of Fairchild and Richard Petritz at a public forum provided by a Financial Times of London/Mackintosh Consultants conference, 'Tomorrow in Electronics', early in 1979. Dr Hogan commented that the 'volume production will no longer go to the world's most complex chip. It will go to the chip that reduces the total systems cost most.' He argued that this will dictate a profound change in company structure. He then argued that vertically-integrated electronics companies will become the order of the day. As Hogan put it 'vertical integration from component design through system manufacture and sale appears to be the main requisite.'

The opposing argument, which is the Intel, Zilog and Inmos argument, is that cost has always been the prime requisite and large end-users will continue to seek ways of sourcing their circuits at the lowest possible price. The in-house manufacturer, so this argument goes, where a vertically-integrated company makes comparatively small batches of circuits, will never be able to compete in price terms with high volume independents making standard processors, memories and microcomputers.

So the battle lines are drawn between vertical integration and mass-production. Hogan predicts that 'ten years from now there will be no large pure semiconductor companies surviving.' Dr Petritz, on the other hand, said 'I will bet that ten years from now IBM will be buying in all but its most specialised chips.' Theoretically, these strategies may not be mutually exclusive. In the short-term Petritz could well be right, but later on 'pure' semiconductor manufacturers could well be absorbed into larger groupings, partly as a result of the rising need for 'designer interaction', between the circuit builder and the end-user to the probable profit of both.

The semiconductor industry has been called the most competitive industry since the industrial revolution: that is why the sheer availability, reliability and cheapness of its products is forcing a new 'heartland' technology on the business world in general.

References

28. Roberts, Derek, *Chips-Challenges and Opportunities*, New Scientist, (London) June 8, 1978.
29. Braun and MacDonald, *Revolution in Miniature*, Cambridge University Press.
30. Orme, M., *Inmos-Mixing Memory and Desire*, Datalink, November, 1978.

8 Silicon futures

"most electronic controls will replace primitive electro-mechanical controls, which are bits of bent wire or something."

Dr Iann Barron

The general characteristics of silicon products

In marketing terms the border line in the microelectronics sector between 'market-pull' and 'invention-push' is hard to discern.[31] More than most innovations, the transistor had been born out of scientific discovery, but early on in the commercial life of the transistor, technology had tended to take over from the emphasis on scientific research and 'market-pull'; and the ability of semiconductor products to create their own markets became increasingly important. So, in essence, through the 1960s and 1970s, the semiconductor business had swung over to 'technology-push'. That push is now so intense that integrated circuits not only have to create markets themselves but also alter technologies in related fields. This latter is where a host of problems, actual and potential occur.

At the same time as semiconductor devices become ever more reproducible and complex (although no one cares to guess at what level of complexity production yields will be lowered), the focus in electronic componentry has been very much on digital rather than analogue devices. This is why the microelectronic revolution is about computing: digital computing, more than anything else. But, ironically, it is likely in its early stages to be a computer revolution that will offer cheap computing power which will not be fully used.

This is about all that is clear. This is probably the most discernible trendline in electronics. A consistent theme of this book has been the fundamental unpredictability of the electronic future, and therefore of the commercial and social changes which will result from any sharp increase in the technology's pervasiveness. The mass-consumer markets so far opened up by SIC technology offer little guide to the future. Each, whether it be the calculator, digital watch or TV game, has been a high circuit-content product, where electronic components have not really had to coexist with robuster mechanical or electromechanical traditions and where the companies offering the products have not had to build up from scratch elaborate back-up infrastructures. Each of the products has been offered to consumers, or in the first instance to retail stores, without any preconceived notion about the particular product's charisma.

There are, as we have seen, three main forces in contention in the marketplace for electronic products:

- The consumers' thirst, especially in the USA, for electronic gadgets, which are often 'impulse' purchased and often so purchased during the Christmas shopping spree. These electronic goods are primarily 'playthings' or utilities, which are 'dedicated' to specific functions and which do not tend to be used, therefore, as general-purpose computers or to be 'tied-in' to other pieces of equipment or appliances. This implies that, despite the functional flexibility offered by microprocessors compared to earlier LSI circuits, mass demand in the early 1980s, at least, will tend to be for 'dedicated' and comparatively simple electronic products, despite the low-cost computing power which is now available. It is not yet the case, for instance, that the definition of a 'liberal education' includes computer programming capabilities;
- The need for semiconductor makers, operating against the industry's 'learning curve' to find mass-market outlets for their increasingly densely-packed circuits. We have mentioned

earlier that the industry's strength (its ability to reproduce complex circuits) is also its Achilles Heel. It is in danger of overproducing circuits which are too complex for most market requirements. The big retail markets for circuits so far — calculators, digital watches and TV games — are too fickle as a basis for a 'highstream' industry like the semiconductor industry. This is why 'home information systems', automotive controls and telecommunications are where most in the industry would like to see the bulk of its production go;
- The resistance of the end-users to complex circuitry. This is not just, as we have seen, myopia on the part of business managements but a shortage of design engineers to design electronic intelligence into products and processes, as well as a shortage of programmers to keep the world's computer population busy, and a lack of cheap mass-produced 'software'.

Thus, whilst as we saw in Table 4.1 (p.69) that the potential applications of microprocessors, associated circuits and the emerging generation of single chip computers spans the entire range of commercial, industrial, consumer and institutional application, the out-turn during the 1980s will be one of selective applications (even if the social and political climate allowed for something broader). It will be some time before most automobile owners will look under their car bonnets like the semiconductor industry electronics engineer and comment scornfully that the engine technology inside 'is old enough to vote'. For all these reasons, we shall confine ourselves in this chapter to a detailed study of the two most likely mass-markets for circuits during the 1980s outside telecommunications, computers and business communications (the last is discussed in the next Chapter):
- low-cost computers for consumers/small businesses;
- automotive controls;

The first major application area of the microprocessor in the consumer market is the low-cost computer. For less than $1000 the consumer can purchase a 'microcomputer' that can run simple programs. This type of computer is sold either as a 'kit' or already assembled: sometimes even preprogrammed. The cheapest microcomputers are those preprogrammed and packaged for a 'dedicated' operation, such as an educational toy or a non-programmable TV game.

The marketing history of the calculator

By far the best example so far of the low-cost computer is the pocket calculator. The pocket calculator not only makes visible the impact of the 'learning curve' on semiconductor components working into end-user products, but it also shows the pervasiveness of semiconductor electronics and the extent to which the consumer market in silicon-based products is a 'black-box'.[32]

The calculator is a computer. Even the most basic calculators do more than simply add, subtract, multiply and divide. By the second half of the 1960s, calculators using sophisticated MOS integrated circuits were available from both Texas Instruments and Mostek, but they aroused little interest.[33] The first US company really to show the way in the market was Universal Data Machines, which operated out of a Chicago warehouse. The company bought its electronic components from Texas Instruments and, using cheap immigrant labour, assembled some 5000 calculators a week for sale at a local department store. Then a Canadian based company, Commodore, which had moved to Silicon Valley, started to assemble calculators using a special technology developed by Bowmar which had previously tried the calculator market itself but withdrawn to become a component supplier. Commodore, like Universal Data, also bought circuits from Texas Instruments.

Between 1971 and 1972 the first mass-produced calculators had halved in price to $50 but still cost less than $20 to assemble. By 1972, Bowmar, seeing the size of the market, struggled to get back into the market it had farmed out and was joined by other semiconductor makers, including Texas Instruments. In the late 1960s and early 1970s, the semiconductor makers had been surprised by the assemblers' component orders and had not thought them justified by the potential in the marketplace. As it turned out, the market potential was there but not as a high value-added operation for the producers as prices tumbled. Soon, as prices fell, the small assembly firms had run into cash flow problems and were incurring bad debts on their component purchases. This combination of factors brought the semiconductor makers into the market.

As a result, in what is now well-known history, the price of the basic, four-function, pocket calculator fell from $100 to $15 in only five years and now stands at around $10. A typical example: a Sharp Electronics Calculator retailed for $395 in 1971. By 1978, a more sophisticated model sold for $10.95. The combination of low price and mathematical capability led to the calculator's acceptance on an unpredicted scale. By 1975, there were nearly 40 million calculators in use in the USA alone. In short, the calculator became what the slide-rule had never been: a mass retail product. The calculator was very much a product which the consumer had not known he wanted until it became available.

The calculator Mark II

The marketing history of the calculator demonstrates graphically the difficulty of marketing electronic goods. The industry is waiting to see whether the next stage up from the calculator (or at least the programmable calculator) will be the personal and small business computer. The first phase of the personal computer's history resembles that of the calculator in some respects. The first company to offer a personal computer 'kit', as we have seen, was MITS. The company was faltering when it announced its 'kit' at the end of 1974 and its managers had no real idea whether people wanted computers. In the event it was found that a lot of people did, even if they were mostly 'hobbyists' initially. By the middle of 1975, several companies were making accessories for the MITS Altair computer. There was also a magazine for 'hobbyists' called *Byte* and soon shops started to mushroom in California, where people could walk in and buy computers, kits and accessories off-the-shelf. By 1978, the fastest growing franchise business in the USA was in computer retail stores. By 1978, there were some fifty brands of personal computers on the market: most of them kits, but some, like the Apple II and Radio Shack's TRS-80, ready-to-use computers.

The computer wares that could be acquired across the counter by 1978 were comparatively rough and ready and the software threadbare and 'do-it-yourself'. The hardware then available was well described as being 'in a state of anticipation'. But Texas Instruments had signalled that it was poised to enter the market to make it respectable and also do to the smaller suppliers of 'hobbyist' kits what it, and other semiconductor manufacturers, had done to the calculator assemblers from 1972 onwards. There was considerable disagreement amongst computer and semiconductor makers about the market potential for small retail computers. For the most part, the semiconductor makers (with the notable exceptions of Texas Instruments and National Semiconductor) had their eye on the business which would result from selling microcomputers as a logic design tool or as evaluation systems to electronics engineers and systems designers. Intel, the company which had pioneered the microprocessor, was still quoting the market size of minicomputers (selling at around $100 000 each) to prove that $1000 computers would never sell in a high enough volume for semiconductor makers to be interested. The mainframe computer makers, for reasons discussed in detail in Chapter 4, were not keen either to move downmarket into such low value-added products. Not surprisingly, the computer industry, which depends so much on its 'software servicing', pours scorn on 'off-the-shelf' software. Nonetheless, over 40 000 computer systems were retailed in the USA in 1977 and by 1978 there were enough Altair and Apple-type machines installed to justify the

Silicon futures 153

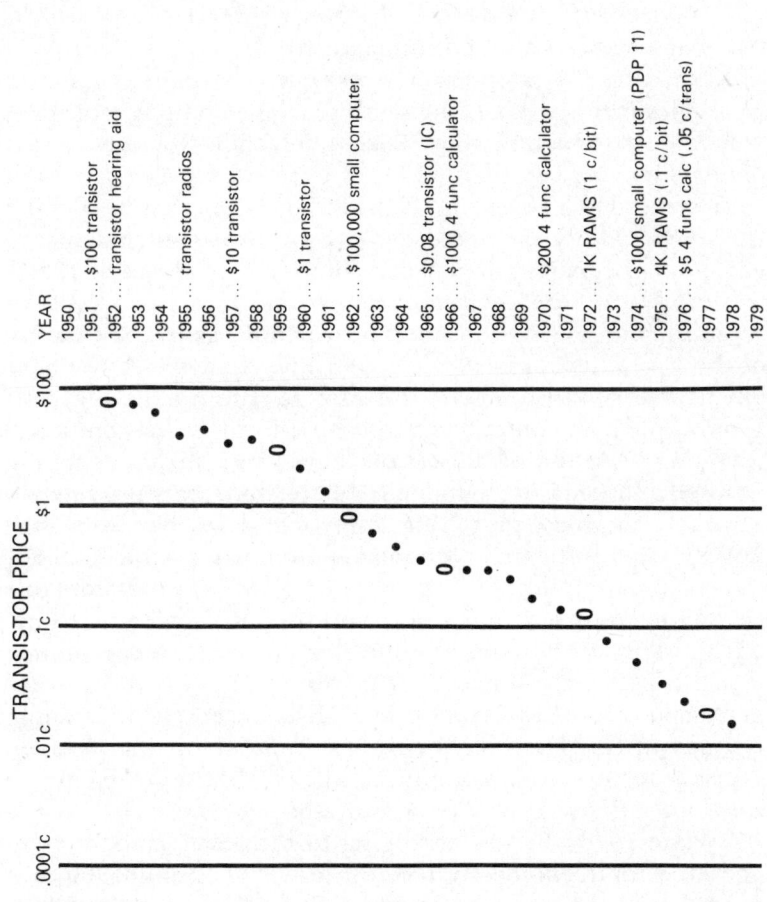

emergence of software publishing companies — selling programs the way record companies sell cassettes. As one leading director of marketing in the home computer business had suggested 'no one would buy a stereo hi-fi if he could not also buy records or tapes to play on it. We will soon see the dawn of a whole new publishing industry.'

According to a market research company, Creative Strategies International, the retail or home computer business will be worth $3.5 billion by 1982, which allows for sales of a lot of machines at less than $1000 a time, and a great deal of software at $10 a program. This kind of prediction lies behind the meticulously planned drive by Texas Instruments to dominate the market in personal computers by the early 1980s. But to turn the personal computer into the kind of reproducible, low-cost business at which TI excels, the nature of the computer business will have to be changed. As we have already seen, 'customised' software to run small, low-cost, general-purpose computers is too high in price for consumers spending less than $1000 on the hardware. TI has therefore devoted a lot of effort to making the software mass-producible. Probably the most promising approach so far has been with 'solid state software'. Modules containing semiconductor memories are plugged into the back of a programmable calculator to turn it into a powerful special purpose machine. TI hopes to use plug-in modules for all its small computers, which it believes will make them easy enough for the average person to use. At the same time, TI has been giving training courses at its Houston Learning Center for businessmen wanting to buy small computers without having to incur the costs of a DP department or consultants.

By late 1978, TI was arranging to introduce computers to operate with the home TV receiver priced at around $400 with small business computers in the $700—$900 range to follow later, containing larger data storage to handle such items as inventory. The small business machines were being designed to be sold off-the-shelf at retail stores and business equipment dealers, and to operate with plus-in software modules with self-instructing programs.

Silicon futures 155

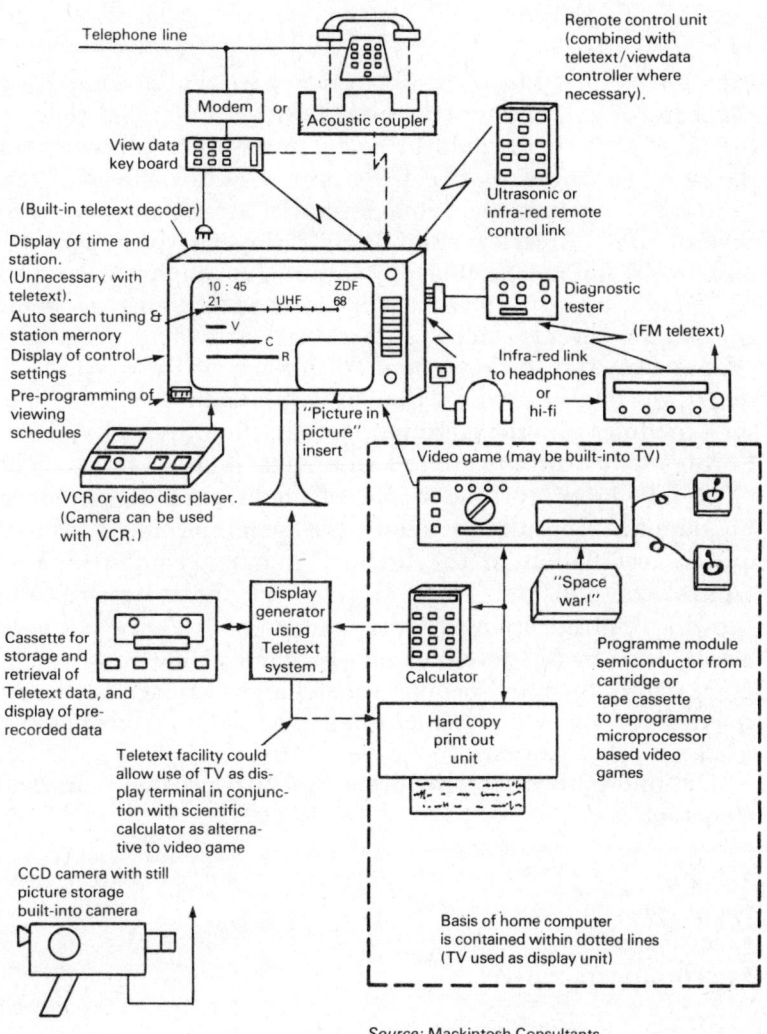

Source: Mackintosh Consultants

Figure 8.1 The home of the future

Lots of computers in the home

Professor John Westcott, head of the department of computing and control at London's Imperial College, estimated that by the mid-1980s there could be seven to ten microprocessors in the average home in the USA and Western Europe. The Arthur D. Little study, cited several times already, predicts that by 1987 American and West European consumers will possess 400 million 'intelligent' modules, at roughly $50 a time in today's dollars, incorporated into such items as home computers, ovens, video games, viewdata and electronic telephones. ADL reckons that 275 million of these will be in the USA. It also predicts that by 1987 annual shipments of such modules into the consumer area in the USA and Western Europe will run at around the 400 million mark. The electronic layout of the home of the future suggested by Mackintosh Consultants shows the potential for advanced circuit installation in the home through a combination of control consoles/and TV/hi-fi/video telephone systems. The growing sophistication of video games for instance has been exemplified by the development of a game centre consisting of eight games for blind people; tone changes replace the screen making for games like paddle ball, and synthesised speech is used for other games.

The microprocessor provides a link between four different elements:

- logic;
- patterns;
- actuators;
- environment sensors.

It is obvious therefore how extensively microprocessor-driven systems can be used. They can, for instance, monitor prevailing weather conditions, forecast future heating needs and adjust room temperatures to this information and also to the living pattern within the household. This is of obvious importance with the high cost of fuel. Similarly, dedicated microprocessors with sensor inputs and outputs such as BIO, RINSE, HOLD and FAST WASH can control washing machines. Again: a microcomputer may perform such routine household tasks as menu planning, taking dietary programmes into account. Digital controls and timers can be used in cooking for displays, while a stored program can provide information on the cooking time necessary for various types of dish as well as automatically turn various burners or ovens on and off in response to program control. A comparatively frivolous example of microprocessor use in the home may occur in the door chime. The cost of a mechanical door chime rises steeply as the number of musical notes is increased (each tubular bell and hammer costs a significant amount in relation to the total) but the microprocessor acting together wth a very modest memory circuit can generate a large repertoire of possible tunes each time the door bell is operated.

The 'intelligent' phone

Perhaps the biggest impact of all will be on the telephone receiver. In the USA, the Carter phone decision and the Federal Communications Commission's (FCC) ruling to permit telephone subscribers to buy their own telephone instruments promises to transform the home telephone. Motorola invested $20 million to develop a microprocessor-operated portable phone weighing less than 2lb, while ITT has blended a phone with a radio alarm clock. Some marketing strategists estimate that the US phoneset market could swell to $1 billion a year in sales by the early 1980s. Texas Instruments estimates that the market in personal communications will reach $3 billion by 1985. TI is placing considerable emphasis on the electronic telephone with a built-in autodialer. AT&T itself, faced with competition in the phoneset market, was, by 1978, looking into micro-applications that would turn the family phone into both fire and burglar alarm as well as intercom system.

Locked into the home

Thus the semiconductor and equipment companies are entering the potentially huge market to provide the phonesets and systems to turn the telephone system into a personal link between every home, and, eventually, perhaps, for linking any two or more individuals wherever they may be. This would transform the use and amount of data flowing into and out of the home, perhaps presented on a television screen and organised by a small computer. Shopping and banking transactions could be done from the home, meters would be read automatically, faults in electronic systems and various domestic appliances diagnosed by remote control. One effect of this would be to make it less and less necessary for people either to retain money or to go out into the streets with money. This could have a marked impact on security firms and police activities since it would eliminate payroll theft and other acts of larceny involving cash. There might also be much less incentive to go out to work or to visit friends when contact and information were so readily available in the home. This would, it it happens, have a marked effect for instance on transport industries and taxi services.

Who wants sophisticated electronics?

The Mackintosh home of the future shows what is possible. But marketing executives and corporate planners must decide what consumers will actually want and what they will resist. No one knew, for instance, to take a simple example, whether consumers would want digital watches, because it was hard to see why most people would need watches which are accurate to within a few seconds a month. There was also some concern that consumers would be put off by the fact that the watches would need new batteries every few months. In the event there was a considerable demand for digital timepieces. But the uncertainties today about the range of sophisticated systems potentially on offer are far greater. We have already mentioned, several times, the controversy over the pace at which 'computer literacy' is likely to spread and the problems of developing adequate, yet cheap, control software.

Programs or dedication?

By 1980 or 1982, at the latest, the success or otherwise of the 'home' computer in the retail market will point to the shape of the future of electronics in the home. In the comparatively near future virtually every device or appliance costing over $50 (and many costing less) will contain computer components. The test will be whether they are treated as computers. As with the washing machine, cited above, most devices will be programmed to behave in specific ways. For instance, the Cadillac automatic 'trip computer' has its own fixed repertory of behaviours, as does the portable telephone-memoriser. But each locks the user in. They are not integrated. If, however, the signs are that personal computers are being used to perform a unifying function — that is, both keeping the records *and* orchestrating the accessories — then distributed computing rather than 'dedicated' microprocessing will need to be a part of new products visualisation by the mid-1980s.

The age of the utility

There are good reasons for suggesting that the reverse may happen. We have already mentioned that there is strong school of thought which believes that the public will remain electronically rather than computer-minded in the foreseeable future. In the final tally, computer manufacturers and appliance manufacturers will build what people are prepared to buy. Probably so long as people buy cameras that they do not understand and hi-fi sets with knobs and switches that cannot be distinguished by touch, they will tend to buy electronic 'utilities'. Different considerations may apply to block the development of the consumer market in telephone appliances. It is too early to know yet whether most people will want to be too easily contactable on the telephone. It may become a consideration similar in kind to fears about swelling computer databanks and their effect on privacy, and the scope for electronic surveillance and subversion. It would almost certainly be premature to take as an emergence of a norm the well-publicised example of Michael Dertouzos, director of the MIT's computer-science laboratory, who uses his home computer to keep all financial data, income tax records, appointments, *aides memoires,* phone numbers and the equivalent of a desk calendar. The Dertouzos children even use the computer to help them compose their Christmas card messages.

Early indications are that the Japanese are basing at least the first phase of their export drive in electronic equipment on simple 'dedicated' electronic products. It is perhaps indicative that during 1977 and 1978 one of the spearheads of that drive into the US market was in cheap electronic cash registers. It is interesting to note too that while Texas Instruments risks considerable resources and kudos on betting on the personal computer market, it is also double-banking by laying considerable stress on simpler electronic devices such as learning aids and electronic dictionaries.

More personal gadgets

The key to this potentially large product market is a single circuit voice synthesiser which TI patented. This was incorporated in TI's successful 'Speak and Spell' product line. The original product stored more than 200 words in the memory circuit. It pronounces a word, and the child, using a keyboard, then attempts to spell it. If the child fails after two attempts, the device says 'that is incorrect' and spells the word out. That learning aid sold for $50. One promising near-term application is in the teaching of foreign languages. According to one expert, the normal operation of the 'learning curve' should lead to 20 000 word products before the 1980s are out. Such voice-synthesising products could extend to such personal aids as dictionaries in all languages which spell words as well as pronounce them, speaking telephone directories, address 'books', and appointment diaries. In short, producers in the consumer markets face similar problems to those faced by semiconductor makers supplying complex components to end-users. These centre on avoiding the temptation to exercise technical virtuosity for its own sake, and supplying usable products which cater for the bulk of mass-market requirements. Due to the forces at work in the electronic component industry, many end-users will have to supply mass-market needs with low-cost volume-produced goods.

The automobile

The use of microprocessors as on-board vehicle controllers is one of the most publicised and potentially significant applications of semiconductor technology. As early as 1969, it had been hoped that within five years all of the USA's ten million new cars would incorporate advanced control circuits. Microprocessors have long been used for such activities as controlling automatic windows and stereo equipment in cars, but it will still not be until the early 1980s that the motor industry becomes a billion dollar customer for the circuit builders. The main reasons for the delay, so far, have been:

- Lack of consumer demand for electronic controls in autos (although in Europe there has long been substantial business in electronic ignition controls and accessories as optional extras). This persuaded Detroit that the introduction of electronics would do nothing to make their products more

attractive: an important consideration in an industry which costs its production to the nearest 1/100th of a penny.
- Fears that electronic components would not be able to function for years in noisy, dirty and hot motor engines, plus slow progress in 'sensor' technology.
- A servicing network in which repair mechanics know about engines with moving parts but nothing about electronics.
- Huge and costly (in replacement cost terms) production lines.
- Concern at the speed of change in the semiconductor industry's technology. The motor industry has to live with the changes it makes for years, and therefore does not want to buy a technology which may soon become obsolete.

But now, as one leader in the semiconductor industry pointed out in late 1977, 'Detroit has been legislated into using electronics as well as into producing lighter vehicles'. Most semiconductor executives, after years of false starts, expect autos to become a billion-dollar market for microprocessors in the early 1980s. This means a lot of microprocessors bulk bought by Detroit at less than $2 a time.

The use of microprocessors is part of what a top executive at Chrysler called a $70 billion race opening up between the motor manufcturers in the USA over a five-year period to design new cars to satisfy the requirements of the law and growing customer demands. This same executive saw 10 per cent of the cost of an automobile in electronic components by 1985. Chrysler itself has been working for some years on the use of microprocessors to monitor and control all the mechanical parts of a car, using a team and facilities once financed by NASA. Initial moves have been to introduce electronics via such gadgets as the completely electronic instrument panel, giving much more information than conventional displays. For instance, the Ford Continental Mark V offered an option called 'miles to empty'. At the push of a button, the driver received a readout of the amount of fuel in the tank and how many more miles he could expect to go, at the same average speed, before a refill was required. But the main areas of development research have been:

- ignition timing;
- exhaust gas recirculation;
- fuel usage measurements;
- automatic braking and blind driving aids.

Transforming the car engine

The operation of a car engine requires a complex matching of engine speed, petrol and air flow and ignition timing. The only way early cars could handle this was through an advance and retard mechanism. Even in the late 1970s, some cars have manual chokes. Eventually these manual controls were replaced by mechanical ones, but even so these could only approximate the required function. But as a result of the introduction of exhaust emission regulations in the USA, massive expenditures have been incurred, as cited above, to introduce chemical and mechanical improvements. By sensing the external environment and computing the required actions, the microprocessor can provide a closer and hence more efficient control over the car engine.

One of the industry's top transmission designers sees the next generation of petrol engines as being like aircraft piston engines: relatively large and efficient with a small working range running weak fuel mixtures at slow speeds, with the throttle wide open. As in the jet engine — the pilot does not dictate the amount of fuel being used — so with the microprocessor-controlled car engine, the driver will only command the speed and performance of the vehicle on the highway but not the engine speed, transmission or sparks.

The GM check list

In the early 1970s, General Motors drew up a detailed check list of microprocessor applications in the automobile. The list

Figure 8.2 The GM micro checklist

Proposed automotive electronic systems

System		Major Development required				Major Barrier		
		Transducer	Processor	Actuator	Display	Cost	Technical	Other
Automatic door locks				×		×		
Alcohol detection systems		×			×	×	×	×
Flasher control systems				×		×		
Programmed driving controls			×	×		×	×	
High speed warning						×		
High speed limiting				×		×		
Lamp monitor systems		×				×		
Electronic horn						×		
Crash recorder		×	×		×	×	×	×
Traffic controls		×	×	×	×	×	×	×
Tyre pressure monitor		×				×		
Tyre pressure control		×		×		×	×	
Automatic seat positioner						×		
Automatic mirror control		×		×		×	×	
Automatic icing control		×				×	×	
Road surface indicator		×			×		×	
4-Wheel anti-lock				×		×		
Vehicle guidance		×		×		×	×	×
Station Keeping	Radar	×		×		×	×	
	Infra red	×		×		×	×	
	Laser	×		×		×	×	
	Sonic	×		×		×	×	
Automatic Brakes	Radar	×	×	×			×	
	Infra red	×	×	×			×	
	Laser	×	×	×			×	
	Sonic	×	×	×			×	
Predictive Crash Sensors	Radar	×				×	×	
	Infra red	×				×	×	
	Laser	×				×	×	
	Sonic	×				×	×	
Electronic timing						×		

Silicon futures

System / Transducer	Major development required				Major Barrier		
	ducer	Processor	Actuator	Display	Cost	Technical	Other
Multiplex harness systems			×		×		
Electronic transmission control			×		×		
Electronic cooling sys. control			×		×		
Closed loop emission control	×		×		×	×	
Accessory power control	×		×		×		
Cruise control			×				
Theft deterrent systems	×				×		
On board diagnostic systems	×				×		×
Off board diagnostic systems	×				×		×
Leveling controls	×		×		×		
Radio frequency display					×		
Digital speedometers				×	×		
Digital tachometers				×	×		
Elapsed time clock				×	×		
Electronic odometer				×	×		
Trip odometer				×	×		
Destination mileage				×	×		
Miles per gallon	×			×	×		
Miles to go	×			×	×		
Estimated arrival time				×	×		
Trip fuel consumption	×			×	×		
Average speed				×	×		
Average miles per gallon				×	×		
Digital fuel gauge				×	×		
Service interval				×	×		
Digital temperature gauges				×	×		
Digital pressure gauges				×	×		
Digital voltmeter				×	×		
Digital metric conversions				×	×		
Acceleration gauge	×			×	×		
Drunk drivers	×	×				×	×
E.K.G.	×	×	×		×	×	×
Sleep detectors	×	×				×	×

Source: General Motors

indicated the number of major developments required before most such systems could become feasible, as well as the current barriers to be overcome. This list is reproduced in Figure 8.2. The problem for the motor industry — something which was not always evident to some understandably impatient semiconductor executives — was that the industry could not just start with a blank sheet and a series of cavalier experiments. What was viewed by some as the result of vast and bureaucratic automobile corporations uninterested in innovation, and by others as simple and perhaps criminal negligence or indolence, was mainly the problem of moving a massive industry, with large mechanised plant, from 'here to there'.

The auto industry 'learning curve'

But now Detroit has been forced into change at a five-year expense of perhaps $70 billion. This is why in 1978 Henry Ford II called the next five years 'the transitional years'. By 1985, according to top planners at General Motors, the world will only have room for six major motor manufacturers — each deploying enormous economies of scale to compete in an increasingly oversupplied market. This market pressure had in 1978 led to Chrysler's sale of its European operations to Peugeot. Chrysler needed the funds to help it finance the $7.5 billion to adapt its products to the legislation, while Peugeot needed Chrysler (Europe) to build a big enough base on which to multisource cheap, standardised components into 2 million European-designed and assembled cars. In the process, competing showroom models would increasingly share exactly the same engines and components.

There is a resemblance here to the background to the semiconductor industry. It may soon no longer be fair to suggest that the semiconductor industry is the most difficult business in the world. Meanwhile, the emerging range of smaller, lighter, cleaner and less fuel-intensive vehicles from Detroit, incorporating electronic controls, means that the USA may well become a major direct exporter of cars by the mid-1980s, provided that the USA's flagging productivity growth rate keeps the dollar at around its 1977-8 parity to other major world currencies. Ford, for instance, may have been impressed by the success of its pan-European model, the Ford Fiesta, but has been caught with the same problem as Chrysler of having to repatriate European earnings and resources to the USA to finance its enforced and bulging investment programme. Meanwhile, General Motors aims to market its 'world car' — the 'J' model — by late 1981.

References

31. Curnow and Freeman, *Product and Process Change Arising from the Microprocessor Revolution and Some Economic and Social Issues,* Sussex University, Science Policy Research Unit, 1978.
32. McWhorter, Eugene W., *The Small Electronic Calculator,* Scientific American, March 1976.
33. Macintosh I.M., *Dominant Trends Affecting the Future of the Semiconductor Industry,* Radio and Electronic Engineer, February, 1973.

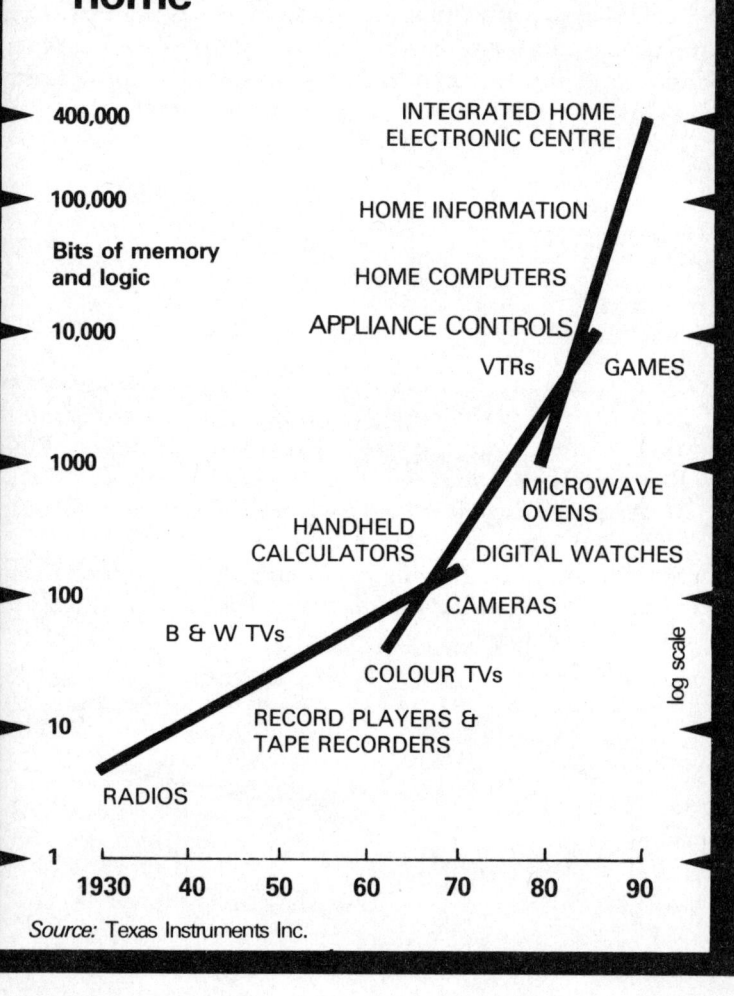

Appendix 8.1: The reinvention of the telephone and the TV receiver

As we saw from the Mackintosh picture of the home of the future both the telephone and the TV receiver are being transformed. Each is being turned by electronic componentry into a communications terminal.

The telephone

Already the telephone can offer a range of sophisticated services to the subscriber. For instance, 'call waiting': the telephone can tell the subscriber when there is another caller on the line by emitting a gentle bleep which only the subscriber can hear. There is also 'call forwarding', under which all incoming calls can be transferred to another number at a location where the subscriber either intends to be or where messages can be taken. 'Speed calling' makes it possible to reach numbers frequently dialled by dialling only a few digits.

But once electronic phonesets are linked into a fully electronic network, which include electronic switching and stored-program control, a range of dramatic new capabilities will be available, which will make the telephone the principal organising agent in the ordering of the information society. That is, unless or until satellite transmissions via wrist-devices take over, which NASA scientists suggest might happen by the year 2000.

Amongst the new telephone services which will probably become available during the 1980s, in areas where the all-electronic network has been installed:

- Telephones which, if instructed, will automatically carry on dialling engaged numbers until the line is free and then let the subscriber know that the number is no longer engaged;
- telephones which can be instructed to accept 'collect' calls from certain pre-selected telephones without involving a human operator;
- by keying in personal identification numbers it will be possible for subscribers to have calls charged to their own telephones, irrespective of where they are making the calls;
- incoming calls from pre-selected numbers will be identified by distinctive ringing patterns, so that the subscriber can decide whether to take the call or not, according to the time he or she has available, his mood or his other priorities dictate;
- electronic tones will alert callers when the voice they are about to hear is recorded.

These are simply some of the personal conveniences which will emerge from the application of electronics to telephones and telephone networks. But more dramatic possibilities are in prospect which were outlined by AT&T's director of network planning to a Congressional committee. He said

> 'undoubtedly, most homes will boast of having a telecommunications center with the capacity to send and/or receive voice, data, graphics, visual information. From this center, a person might perform a host of other functions that require that he or she physically leave home. If, as some have suggested, people will not accept such homebound

confinement, then work might be performed in nearby work centers. In any event, future communications will make it possible to simulate the benefits of large-city living without having to go to the large city.'

All current predictions about the use of home computers, whether for education, entertainment, information gathering or shopping, involve a linkup with the telephone system. The versatility and ubiquity of telecommunications will be based entirely on microelectronics.

The television set

Like the phoneset, the TV receiver is being transformed by a range of microelectronic components. Progressively, during the 1980s, viewers will be able to program evenings and days of their own choosing by operating their TVs as communications terminals, and they will sooner or later get accustomed to the idea of paying for some of the services which they call onto their screens. Amongst the developments in TV which will be chanced and exploited over the next decade are these:

- home video recorders, which can tape up to four hours of programmes off the air which people can watch at their own discretion, or which can play shop-bought prerecorded tapes;
- portable video cameras for home-made productions;
- video disc players, whose programme comes in the form of 12-inch metallised records;
- electronic data transmission, giving the viewer the ability to call up on the screen a wide range of printed material, such as news reports, market information or reference matter;

- pay TV delivered either over the air on specially licensed stations or cable TV systems;
- two-way TV, allowing the viewer to respond to and interact with the TV broadcast by sending digital signals to the transmission centre on a return wire. This has had a famous tryout at Columbus, Ohio, in the innovation known as Qube;
- satellite transmission, making national and regional distribution of programmes available to film studios, advertisers, syndicators and other entrepreneurs: thus breaking the networks' control over the mass market;
- fibre optic wiring which can increase a hundredfold the number of channels on a television set.

During the next decade two general developments are inevitable:

- the number of channels a TV set can receive will expand;
- dozens of new and relatively low-cost routes for programme distribution via satellites will be available.

9 Networks to the future

> "all around us, tangibly and materially, the thinking envelope of the earth — the noosphere — is adding to its internal fibres and tightening its network."
>
> *Teilhard de Chardin*

Potentially even more significant than the use of electronics in the automobile (which could well lead to automatic piloting and computerised traffic controls) is what is in some respects the counterimpact to physical transport of microelectronics on computer networking. As we saw in the section on *telematics* in Chapters 2 and 4, the common use of electronic components, i.e. 'logic-gates' and microprocessors in both data processing and data transmission is merging the hitherto separate technologies underlying the telephone and computer industries into a single technological mode. In commercial and social terms this may make the first thirty years of electronic data processing look like a warm-up. Amongst other things, it promises to transform the office. The 1970's will probably be deemed the decade of the microprocessor, whereas the 1980s will almost certainly become the era of the information network.

A $400 billion information industry

It is this mix of the telephone and computer industries to create new information systems based on communications networks that will lead, eventually, to integrated information systems for business corporations, practical electronic funds' transfer systems for banks and retailers and to the so-called office of the future. Executives in both the supplier industries in the USA (where the scene has been opened up to competition, in particular by the FCC's decision to allow telephone subscribers to buy their own phone instruments), expect the emerging 'information services' industry to generate annual revenues of nearly $400 billion by the early 1990s, and to grow in sales terms by 15 to 20 per cent a year throughout the next decade. This sales figure is the result of an analysis of potential 'displacement costs' for transportation, data collection, use of paper and energy in more than sixty market sectors. This displacement cost analysis points to the impact of the prospective merger of data processing and data transmission, under the influence of the semiconductor industry 'learning curve'. The first clear implication of the force of that 'learning curve' is the recognition that the $30 billion world computer industry will progressively shift its emphasis from large central host computers to terminals (especially 'intelligent' terminals) and towards small communicating computers. This means that the distinction between computers and such items of office equipment as business exchanges, dataspeed terminals, facsimile machines, telephones and telex equipment will become less clear. The second major impact of the fall in electronic component prices is that the cost of the equipment and services required for computer networking brings it within the scope of a wide range of businesses. By 1985, International Data Corporation sees data communications revenues exceeding data processing revenues at the $100 billion a year mark, but that may reflect the increasing merger of DP into data transmission with the DP element getting lost in the classifications.

Computer networks vs roads

This is the background to the idea seriously put forward by computer technologists that computer networks can be a substitute for roads. But as former IBM engineer, James Morris, an acknowledged expert on computer networking, has pointed out, the acceptance of computer networks will largely depend on the price of petroleum. The coming competition in the 1980s between AT&T and companies like ITT and IBM in the *telematic* field is dramatic enough, but the prospective competition between the *telematic* companies and the oil industry and oil producers could be even more dramatic.

What about the price of oil?

At the moment a large proportion of the world's consumption of petroleum is used to transport people who simply want to exchange information. Much of this information could be delivered through computer networks, especially where video telephones and confravision could be operated. This applies to sales teams as well as to executives travelling to offices to gain access to information or secretarial services as well as to attend meetings. Already in the USA, computer networks, particularly Telenet, have posed a challenge to the physical transport of surface mail, since much business information can be either put, or converted via modems, into digital form for computer data transmission.

But the price of petroleum is as difficult to gauge as the impact on any cross-competition between computer networks and petroleum-based transport. For instance, in the autumn of 1978 most petroleum experts had talked of an oil glut during 1979. The 'spot' price of crude oil had drifted downwards through much of 1978 and the world economy was expected to grow less fast in 1979 than it had in 1977 and 1978. However, when the net effect of the Iranian revolution was to reduce the world's daily supply of crude by 2 million barrels against a total world consumption of 57 million barrels in 1978, petroleum experts quickly talked of an oil shortage of crisis proportions. In some quarters, however, it is expected that the power of OPEC could wane during the 1980s with the emergence of powerful non-OPEC oil suppliers such as Mexico and China. Far from an oil shortage, there has been evidence of an appreciable surplus. A study published by the MIT Energy Laboratory suggested the OPEC crude oil price had been fixed in 1973 at $7 to $10 more than the price that would prevail in the competitive market. But OPEC was supported by the world's oil industry which, on the whole, has shown higher revenues following the big OPEC price rise of 1973-4, and by the powerful lobby of the armaments industry which had made huge sales to the Shah's Iran, Saudi Arabia and other mid-East countries.

Moreover, the World Bank, which was studying the background to making loans to developing countries such as India for oil exploration, commissioned a geophysicist with the US Geological Survey, Bernardo F. Grossling, to estimate total global petroleum reserves. Grossling put the figure at 6000 billion barrels — ten times the figure for proven reserves cited by the US administration. The World Bank figure represented nearly 300 years supply at 1978 rates of consumption. Grossling's report went on to suggest that the real costs of oil to be found would be significantly lower than the price set for OPEC oil or by the marginal costs in the USA.

By the late 1980s it is possible that, due to the declining influence of OPEC in total world oil production and countertrades of cheap petroleum with oil suppliers like China and Mexico, the price of oil could look more competitive against the cost of computer networking than seems possible at present.

A huge economic battle

Meanwhile, the computer and telephone industries are making their deployments. The economic stakes are huge. The telephone system (over 90 per cent of which was dominated by AT&T in the USA in 1977) absorbs some 20 per cent of all the external financing raised by US business corporations each year. AT&T argued that the efficient operation of the telephone system required that the company provide all aspects of telecommunication from terminal to terminal. It developed leased-line facilities for data transmission between computers. Increasingly, however, since the mid-1970s, other companies have been providing specialised services, particularly through computer data transmission, through cross-country microwave relay systems; and a number of satellite firms started to transmit computer data, facsimile and TV broadcasts. But by 1978 the microwave and satellite transmission systems had still not become heavy competitors in voice transmission.

Amongst other things, the entry of specialised carriers into the market during the 1980s could create political upheavals in the USA as AT&T's dual pricing structure is undermined. The company had followed the policy of subsidising consumer services, especially to remote areas, by the pricing of its business services. This would be upset were energetic computer companies to offer business services which undercut AT&T services.

But the computer companies and others have started to move. Competition in the 1980s will be intensified by satellite services, particularly from the US Business Systems (SBS) network which is jointly owned by IBM, Comsat and Aetna Casualty and Surety and which received a licence from the FCC to offer leased data communications channels over the USA starting in 1981. This venture, plus others projected by Xerox, ITT and RCA, have very important implications for the whole *telematic* industry across the world.

The age of the satellite

Large satellites can be used at much less marginal cost than the conventional telephone network to send vast quantities of information and broadcasting to rooftop antennae. Moreover their capital cost would be infinitessimal compared to the cost of replacing electromechanical telephone systems with electronic ones. For instance, AT&T is threatened with the premature obsolescence of $120 billion worth of installed telephone equipment, switching devices and wires. Since any large company anywhere in the world could easily put up receiving antennae, satellite systems pose a significant threat to the monopolies of the PTTs in Europe as well as elsewhere in the world. This may be particularly so in Britain, where the PTT is considered to be far too cautious in its management of its monopoly position as a buyer of information technology. The CSERB report cited earlier, co-authored by the Inmos director of strategy, Dr Iann Barron, suggested that the British Post Office (PTT) has shown little appreciation of the consequences of programmed digital electronics and that it probably does not have the expertise or capability to carry through the development of its 'System X' electronic exchange. The report suggests that if this is so, it would effectively destroy the UK telecommunications industry and with it the remainder of the information technology industry. This would make Britain, which is the centre for a large number of US subsidiaries and transnational businesses, a potentially lucrative market for companies like IBM and ITT offering alternative systems.

Japan's glass fibre city

In marked contrast to Britain is Japan, which as we saw in Chapter 1, actually has a technology policy. Japan, for instance, had the world's first town to be completely wired with optical fibres. The fibres themselves, which are made of extremely clear glass, can carry hundreds of ordinary telephone conversations or one video telephone call virtually free of electrical interference. In November 1978 Japan's leading computer company — Fujitsu — unveiled the world's first optical fibre modem for switching messages between computers and their peripheral equipment. This not only cleans up the networks but extends them over longer distances than can ordinary modems.

Japan's experiment at Higashi-Ikoma, which is near Osaka, is funded by companies like Fujitsu, Matsushita, Toshiba and Sumitomo Electric. The Japanese Ministry of International Trade and Industry, MITI, has earmarked some $20 million for the project. Higashi-Ikoma is being used a a testbed for all sorts of industrial applications of optical fibres, which may be a partial alternative or supplement to satellites and conventional telephone systems.

Heartland America

But the USA remains the heartland of the business competition which will largely shape the *telematic* future. A confrontation between IBM and AT&T was inevitable since data processing evolved to include remote terminals, and computer manufacturers had been reluctant to offend AT&T, which was second only to the federal government as a customer for data-processing equipment. But with computer peripherals now accounting for 45 per cent of the computer industry's sales and with more and more items of office equipment becoming computer peripherals and/or stand-alone processors, it was clear that before long industrial logic would force IBM into direct competition with AT&T, and the battle was joined either to 'digitalise' the regulated telephone lines and systems or to transmit data in other ways. At present, with electromechanical switching centers in the ordinary telecommunications system, the international phone system is inadequate for carrying the swelling traffic of computer data at the sort of speeds required — some 50 000 bits (binary digits) per second. This is why many large firms in the USA and Western Europe are setting up their own private, purpose-built, networks, for inter-company data transmission, instead of using the public utility phone wires. In these PABX-based systems, computers act as the switching centers. An example of a technically advanced private network in Europe is British Steel's COTEN system which links 150 terminals around the country to seven remote mainframe computers.

The increasing emphasis on 'intelligent', networked terminals was made evident in the move by the world's largest civilian computing network, the General Electric, GEISCO, which offered 'intelligent' terminals to its customers. Although GEISCO, which involves a network of 150 large, satellite-linked computers, was capable of carrying out any processing required by a customer, it was found that locally processed tasks often worked out to be more economic.

IBM's systems network architecture

Thus, IBM developed the concept of 'systems network architecture', which is a means of defining how an enormous variety of computers and peripheral equipment can communicate with each other. This has uncovered the two main routes of satellites and telecommunications. By 1984-5 IBM hopes to have in operation via its SBS venture private networks using at least 375 earth stations available to large corporations and government agencies in America. In the process, IBM has manoeuvered itself into a very strong position. It is risking at most $500 million in its satellite system, which is only 10 per cent of its 1978 net current cash reserve. But should AT&T work the telephone lines to fend off the IBM competition, Bell would have to introduce a new range of data-communications systems itself, including high-speed channels. That would trigger a surge in computer and office equipment revenues that would sink any losses which IBM might incur with SBS. As a study on IBM/SBS by International Data Corporation put it 'SBS will score as a catalyst in shaping future communications technology.'

Whatever happens, the office is set to be transformed during the 1980s. The shape of the office future in terms of the range of electronic equipment and networks has been set out in detail in both the ADL and CSERB reports. ADL sees the rapid development of new text processing systems, facsimile and copying machines, electronic telephones, dictating systems and communications processors. ADL experts see these plugging into a kind of 'information ring-main' around the office which will enable the different types of equipment to communicate with one another. Ultimately, a letter typed on a keyboard or even dictated to a voice input typewriter in one country may appear on an 'intelligent' copier thousands of miles away in another country. In their CSERB report, Barton and Curnow, isolated the electronic typewriter as the key office device. They suggest that beyond conventional typewriter capabilities it will have word processing, editing and limited calculating faculties, and be able to transmit and receive data through the 'information ring-main'. The ring-main would not only interconnect to specialist office computers and databanks, but also control connections with the external public utility information system. ADL sees the world business communications market reaching annual shipments of $20 billion by 1987, of which the US market would take $13 billion.

Some time ago, IBM estimated that the average per capita investment in the office was only $500 compared to $5000 in the factory. In all circumstances, this opens up the office to electronic automation, with at least 40 per cent of clerical time taken up with such routine tasks as creating records, transcription from manuscript to typescript, filing, indexing, searching, retrieving, copying and distributing records of one kind or another. Implicit in the IBM figures is the far lower replacement cost involved in moving office systems into electronics than manufacturing plant. The prospects in the US office equipment market encouraged Britain's biggest electronics company, GEC, to make an agreed $100 million bid for US office equipment maker A.B. Dick in November 1978. For instance, Arthur D. Little sees US business communications shipments reaching $13 billion a year by 1987. Dick, which produced a range of equipment from franking machines to offset printers, operated in a somewhat different marketplace from IBM and Xerox. The GEC strategy was that by adding its telecommunications and computer resources to Dick's US customer base, it would be able to persuade those customers to move 'components up' into more integrated office systems. The argument used by GEC Chairman, Sir Arnold Weinstock, was that a business does better than average if it can get 2 to 5 per cent of a very large market and simply keep its sales up with the market's overall rate of growth, than it will in having a bigger slice of a slower growing market.

Europe may lag

But a report of the European scene compiled by consultants Pactel suggested that progress in the European market could be comparatively slow and untidy in the electronic office equipment sector. While accepting that the individual components were in place by 1977 to make the integrated office feasible, the report points to three practical problems: the difficulties of linking facsimile machines to computers; the business of sorting out serious from frivolous applications; and the fragmented marketing of competing pieces of equipment which are difficult to mix into a system. Nonetheless, progress is being made in two main areas:

- Facsimile. The main purpose of this process is to send printed messages over the telephone wire. By 1978, machines had been developed that could transmit a page in under a minute, but such machines still cost $10 000. By the mid-1980s, such a machine should only cost the equivalent of one of the 1978 models which took three minutes to transmit a

page of copy. In the USA, ITT was actively engaged with equipment to switch messages between incompatible machines in different companies. In Europe, there has been a considerable problem of intercompany machine incompatibility. But facsimile is, in general, moving into direct competition with the mail service, especially in the USA where some 65 per cent of the first class mail is computer-interactive or machine-generated. (See Appendix 9.1, p.187.)
- Private electronic exchanges. In the early 1970s IBM beat the European equipment makers with the success of its electronic telephone exchange in the $500000 European business exchange market. But the main constraint on the market is that different PTT regulations from country to country mean that equipment has to be designed separately for each country.

Pactel forecast that European office equipment sales would rise from $1.3 billion in 1978 to $2.1 billion in 1986; a considerably more modest rate of growth than forecast for the US market. But, all this will probably be dwarfed by the repercussions of the competition between IBM and AT&T. As we saw at the end of Chapter 6, the onset of the pervasive phase of microelectronics, against a background of a serious shortage of the appropriately qualified design engineers and the gathering shortfall in the world's programming capability, presents formidable potential problems to businesses forced to use the technology by competitors with more adaptable infrastructures. The incipient clash between IBM and AT&T is a case in point, which has been forced by the merger of data-processing and communications technologies as a result of the development of advanced electronic circuitry.

The AT&T case study

The imperative of change forced on AT&T by competition unleashed by FCC rulings on the installation of equipment hooked into the telephone system and the emergence of a single mode technology, represents what has been called 'the greatest challenge in American business'. Not that AT&T is lagging in microelectronics know-how; the Bell Laboratories have a record second to none in electronics research. The challenge is that AT&T has to turn itself into a marketing company. In days past, nurtured in the cosseted environment of regulated monopoly, AT&T's sales approach had been anything but aggressive. In the past, under the Bell 'system', the performance of line executives was measured by a host of artificial indices and productivity measures. For instance, under the traditional net order measurement system, the number of orders each line executive obtained was plotted, but not their revenue contribution. Now Bell marketing executives will be judged on a net revenue basis: how much revenue they bring in and at what cost.

In 1974, AT&T's twenty-three operating companies did not include a single vice-president or director of marketing or sales. Now each has a marketing officer. In 1978, AT&T chairman, John de Butts, went onto the intracompany TV to tell every employee that 'we will become a marketing company'. Between 1973 and 1978, marketing expenditures for the Bell System have more than doubled to top $2 billion. Nearly 2000 managers a year from the Bell operating companies have attended special marketing courses arranged at the AT&T headquarters. By mid-1978, in a major break with tradition, AT&T recruited over 100 systems analysts from outside, including IBM and Xerox. The tradition had always been that all promotion took place from within, on the premiss that nobody who had not been brought up with the 'system' could understand it. One of these outsiders was Archie McGill, a director of marketing and development, who was hired from IBM, where at 33 he had been the youngest vice-president in IBM's history. In its field corps, AT&T tried to match IBM's strength by hiring several hundred recruits from suppliers of data-processing equipment.

The extent of the change, as far as the old guard at AT&T was concerned, was expressed by deButts when he told a Senate subcommittee in 1977 that 'the service motivation has been bred in the bones of the telephone people over the course of a hundred years. To supplant that motivation with a market motivation might make us no less profitable a business... But we would be a different business surely, and I for one cannot help but feel that we would be the poorer for it and so would the public we serve.'

The case study of AT&T, although in many respects unique, points to the magnitude of change which will be forced on managers of all kinds of businesses, if and when competitors better prepared than they in infrastructure terms enter the marketplace with products and services based on advanced electronic circuits.

Conclusions

The onset of *telematics* has almost endless potential consequences for the world business community. Not only does it present the prospect of direct or indirect competition between the petroleum and electronics industries by the late 1980s, but also the huge tussle between AT&T and IBM in the USA. As international businesses offering 'systems', such as IBM, ITT and Xerox, launch communications satellites, the monopoly positions of some of the world's major PTTs will be threatened, and businesses will have the difficult choice of whether to link their information systems to conventional telephone systems or to satellite or microwave transmission.

The clear implication is that computing devices will become extremely widespread and 'unimportant'. The mere processing of data will be taken for granted because it will be both cheap and widely distributed in relation to a business's equipment system as a whole. Much more important will be the computer networks and terminals used to gain access to them. This is why IBM is poised to lever its huge customer base into computer networks and the automated office. Some side effects of this drive could be to leave privately-controlled communications satellites to transmit the bulk of the world's business and government data and broadcasting. At the same time, both the transport industries and postal services could be severely hit as *telematics* become an alternative to physical mobility. But in the emerging business scene of the 1980s, those companies which fail to develop comprehensive, transmittable databases will be uncompetitive in vital areas such as information about themselves and their operating environments. As the industrialised world moves into a post-industrial phase, information becomes the most important factor of production. This is at the root of the symbolic battle between IBM and AT&T. The computer networks of the 1980s will be to the electronics revolution what canals, roads and railways were to the first industrial revolution. It was estimated in 1973 that to answer the calls of the knowledge industry by 1988-9, electronic systems (in terms of number and processing capacity) would have to increase a hundredfold. That is why *telematics* is the 'heartland' business of the 1980s, just as microelectronics is the 'heartland' technology.

Appendix 9.1: Electronic mail

It is estimated that in most industrialised countries some 65 per cent of the first class mail is computer interactive or machine generated. Thus electronic transmission becomes highly feasible. Mail can be sent by facsimile for long-distance transmission. 'Telewriters' connected to telephones can transcribe telephone messages into written form. Mail can be sent coded or decoded and routed to home terminals. Delivery of newspapers and magazines by facsimile has been feasible since the early 1960s. Teletext systems are also technically in place under which information can be transmitted daily and then stored in the electronic memory of the user's TV receiver. The user can then select the appropriate page for whatever item he wants when he wants it by operating a simple keyboard. Alternatively, there is 'Viewdata' under which information is transmitted by telephone but displayed on a terminal screen. The Yankee Group of consultants, for instance, has estimated that by 1982 two-thirds of the 500 biggest companies in the US will have internal electronic mail.

The basic hardware of electronic message systems (EMS) already exists: the telephone. At the same time, the facsimile process had been speeded up by electronic technology especially under the spur of the Japanese who had to get round the problem that their language cannot be sent from a computer keyboard but requires the graphics process of facsimile. By definition, telephone messages are a form of EMS, but the crucial point for modern industry and commerce is to be able to send and print hard copy in seconds. This hard copy capability — more permanent than a business conversation and faster than the mail — is the heart of a growing issue around which huge business interests are deployed.

The speed with which EMS develops will be largely determined by human attitudes; by how quickly the older generation of executives and current status pressures work against executives accustomed, on an increasing scale, to issue orders directly into a computer terminal.

A significant compromise between the traditional system of hand-delivery of mail and EMS has just been offered by the US Postal Service, with its new customer billing service for major corporations. The Postal Service is guaranteeing to transmit, fold and envelope, as well as hand deliver by letter carrier, monthly credit card bills anywhere in the USA in two days at most and one day in most cases. The Postal Service will use its computer system to receive computerised customer accounts from the client-list corporations and then to organise the printing, folding and enveloping and delivery of the letters at twenty-five printing and delivery centres run by Western Union.

EMS, whether it be the activities of the US Postal Service, the selling of facsimile machines, or the use of satellites for message transmission, promises to be a swelling business in the 1980s and an important time-saving or productivity factor for most business executives.

Appendix 9.2: Satellites: business uses space technology

During the 1980s, possibly the most competitive commercial battle of all will intensify over computer networks and be focused on whether the networking of the information society should be based on the telephone system or communications satellites. Technically, the future should probably lie with satellites but political considerations may block the full exploitation of satellites. Indeed, in the late 1960s the Bell laboratories researchers had concluded that a few powerful satellites of advanced design could handle far more traffic than the entire AT&T long-distance network. But AT&T was blocked from acting by the FCC and was forced to spend billions of dollars and years improving its terrestrial network, which it saw as potentially uncompetitive.

The current generation of satellites measure 10 feet across, and are used extensively for surveillance and meteorology as well as broadcasting. But satellites measuring thousands of feet in diameter are in prospect with the anticipated advent of the space shuttle in late 1979. Thus space technology will permit the construction and orbiting of communications satellites with much larger antennas, far greater total power, utilising microprocessors and complex networks of interconnecting switches. Such satellites would be able to complete microwave links between huge numbers of small, low-power terminals on the ground — even down to devices as small as wrist watches. In cost terms considerable progress has been made. The earth station for Early Bird, the first commercial satellite, cost $10 million. A powerful station today costs less than $100,000. The combination of large, powerful, micro-electronically-controlled satellites with a large number of ground terminals opens up the following prospects:

- electronic mail distribution by satellite. Single satellites of the capacity envisaged in the 1980s could handle up to a 100 billion pages a day — larger than the entire current postal system. Letters could still be written, collected and delivered in the conventional way, but copied by TV-scanners and transmitted via satellites;
- a vast extension of information services. Access to public libraries and information banks, film and entertainment libraries could be obtained by subscribers possessing simple 3-foot antennas and transmitters resembling citizens' band radio;
- vehicles and packages, with small radio devices attached to them, could be monitored by satellite. The same principle could be used for global search and rescue operations.

But the most startling prospect of all, which is seriously suggested by space scientists at NASA, is the use of satellites in holography. This opens up the prospect of stay-at-home travel. Under this concept, completely lifelike, three-dimensional images in colour can be transmitted from one place to another by the use of satellite-linked laser illuminators, relay cameras and laser projectors. This means, for instance, that conferences can be held in several locations, in each of which the individual or group can review reports, examine solid models from different angles and indulge in all the usual transactions of a conference, except perhaps for shaking hands.

These are some of the notions which lie behind the IBM satellite-based 'office of the future' and Xerox's, 'X ten' system.

Epilogue: Computers break loose: the emergence of the UIM

> "whatever you feed into the machine on subliminal level the machine will process — So we feed in "dismantle thyself..."
>
> *William S. Burroughs*

The essential theme of this book has been the way in which 'quantum leaps' in component technology have transformed the computer.[34] Not only has computer power increased roughly tenfold every eight years since 1946 — as the componentry has shifted through four generations: from vacuum tube, transistor, simple integrated circuit to densely-packed LSI and soon VSLI circuits — but also the size and cost of computers has shrunk dramatically too. This is why, as the *Economist* has noted, 'to ask what the applications are is like asking what are the applications of electricity'. The richness of the future is pointed up when it is recognised that, at the time of the first generation of vacuum tube computers in 1947, the US Department of Commerce predicted that the installation of a hundred computers in the USA would satisfy all US electronic data-processing requirements.

The fifth generation of computers, built out of such devices as bubble memories and superconducting Josephson junctions, will be on the market in the 1980s. By the late 1980s IBM scientists see the prospect of tiny computers refrigerated in tanks of liquid helium which will be at least a hundred times faster than today's machines. The sixth generation, which may be designed and ready to go by the end of the decade, may usher in what has been called the ultra-intelligent machine

(UIM). These machines could lead to such spectacular advances in artificial intelligence that they are scarcely an appropriate topic for this book. Dicbold Research forecasts that by 1990 a computer processor will be available which has twenty-five times the power of an IBM 370/168 (one of the most powerful) at the same cost.

As we have seen, the drive to use microelectronics to make the personal computer a winner in the marketplace, involves radical changes in the basis of computing centred on making programming mass-producible. But the basis of computing is changing in an even more profound way because of the change in the basic computer components which lie behind the exponential growth in computer power.

The change in computing was delineated by the remarkable John Von Neumann back in 1951 at the now famous Hixon Symposium. Von Neumann's concern was the nature of the 'complex' machine: that is, a machine made up of 10^4 units, which compares with 10^{10} neurons in the cortex (thinking part) of the brain. In 1951, digital computers were still based on bulky and fragile vacuum tubes and as Von Neumann pointed out at the time, a computer of this 'complexity' would have needed the equivalent of the Niagara Falls to supply the current and the Niagara River to carry away the heat. But at the Hixon Symposium, Von Neumann set out the future. He suggested then that

> 'it is probably not true for most automata of this degree of complexity — 10_4 units — that they are really identical copies of what is on the blue-prints. And it is probably no longer even true that there is anybody around who had anything except an intuitive relationship to it......... as machines get more complex building will become a completely nominal operation, not completely controlled by what one finds in blueprints... it has already happened in industry that in the introduction of mass production you are no longer producing the product but you are producing something which will produce the product...'

As Von Neumann suggested, the relationship between the computer designer and the programmer would become progressively 'looser'.[35] This was evident by the latter part of the present decade. For instance, the astronomer, Dr Carl Sagan, reported that the computer on the Viking Mars lander project had shown signs of breaking loose, even though it had a memory of only 18 000 words. According to Sagan: 'we do not know in all cases what the computer will do with a given command. If we knew, we would say it is 'only' or 'merely' a computer. When we do not know, we begin to wonder if it is truly intelligent.'

Although it remains true to say that a computer is a 'forthright' machine which is the epitome of 'literal-mindedness'; and that a computer will only do what it is programmed to do, even at present levels of machine complexity and processing speeds, the more important issue becomes to what extent the machine will do things the program has not predicted it will do. Today's large computers are quite capable of looking for a solution out of a choice of possible paths and coming up with solutions no human being has spotted. The experiments with chess-playing computers are a significant pointer to the future. At the lower level Dr Arthur Samuel of Harvard taught two IBM computers to play checkers, and to polish their games by playing each other; eventually one of the computers went on to defeat a human champion who had not been defeated for eight years by a human opponent. One of the most advanced experiments with chess-playing computers is the result of a wager between two leading experts in the artificial intelligence field who also happen to be first-rate chess players. The two men, Donald Michie and David Levy, bet $2500 on whether a chess-program would beat Levy.[36] The term of the wager was ten years and although Levy won the bet, it was a near call. A computer has already beaten him at 'blitz chess', and given him tough games, tournament-style. One of the most important computer experiments over the next decade will be to see whether computers can be programmed to enable them to form the really deep plans which are the essence of grand-master chess.

Meanwhile, the ability of the emerging generation of computers to process information and compare propositions so quickly that they can come up with solutions and simulations which no human being has spotted, could have enormous repercussions on human life. No 'highstream' scientist these days, including the medical scientist, operates efficiently without some kind of 'synergistic' relationship with a computer. As this process develops (and it should as the computer 'literacy'[37] of today's high-school and college population is enhanced, if not necessarily expanded dramatically in terms of crude numbers compared to today's computer users), the computer will become much less of a tool and more of an extension of the person working with it: rather as a car is to the experienced and expert driver.

Almost certainly, the combination of increasingly powerful computers with human beings better able to take advantage of them could lead to major breakthroughs in the scientific and social fields as computers help humans to:

- form hypotheses;
- plan critical experiments;
- interpret results.

As we saw in Chapter 2, diagnostic computers are already being used in hospitals to come up with the final diagnosis and silicon electronics is being used as a substitute for damaged neural networks. But just as during the first generation of computers, electronic data processing was largely confined to scientists, so 'synergistic' relationships with computers today are largely confined to the scientific community. However, by the third and fourth generations of computers in the 1960s and early 1970s, computer use extended far beyond the scientific community and the computer had become a widely used business machine. During the 1980s, the ubiquity of computing power is likely to be more and more expertly used by corporate planners, product designers and marketing executives, as such people learn how to use computers. This, as we suggested in Chapter 2, could well transform the business scene in terms of product and service visualisation and in terms of the mechanism of supply and demand; the market will almost certainly start to act much more responsively, as customers' wishes and producers' intentions are registered almost simultaneously. For instance, through Viewdata-type link-ups, consumers may be able to purchase product designs at a deep discount to the price of their final embodiment in finished products six months down the line.

But these very trends towards a 'looser' relationship between computer and systems designers and the machines and programs they create, throw up serious worries and uncertainties: the more so as computers become more ubiquitous. Joseph Weizenbaum of the MIT Computer Science Laboratory worried about the 'literal-mindedness' of computers and their tendency to act unpredictably. It is not simply that computers can now do unpredictable things with their instructions, 'which may be much different from what you had in mind'; it is also that a swelling population of interconnected computers will act on as well as correct programs. One leading computer scientist, D. Raj. Reddy of Carnegie-Mellon University, fears that universally available microcomputers might be used to subvert society by intervening in peoples' relationships with their own computers — for instance, by instructing the other computers to cut off services like the telephone or the bank. There is also the much-stressed danger that computer databanks might be used for the wrong purposes and that governments might eventually possess one immense, interconnecting computer system. This leads to the danger of 'Big Brother' as well as the prospect that the systems might break down or be subject to human error or sabotage. New York has recently experienced the severe dislocations of electricity power cuts, as a limited example of what happens with even greater dependence on computers and computer-related systems.

So far there has been comparatively little attention given to these problems, largely because policy-makers and business planners are having to wrestle full-time with the impact of microminiaturised computing on the way the next generation of products is designed, marketed, made and distributed into the market. But just as the scene becomes clearer over microelectronic applications, these profounder problems will have to be tackled. Such problems as how to isolate government computers from one another; whether the regulatory agencies should allow computers to communicate with each other via unregulated communications satellites; how to check thoroughly the programming of military computers; what back-up system to install; how to balance the growth of databanks and databases with civil liberties and privacy; how to manage a society in which there are no 'insulation spaces' — just to mention a few.

Thus, the quantum jumps in electronic components technology since the late 1940s not only pose a dual threat and opportunity to the business community as the 1980s unfold, but also a dual threat and opportunity to the whole of human society as the computer-information revolution gets truly underway. But this conclusion is somewhat tantological, and tantologies tell us nothing about the world.

References

34. Dolotta, Bernstein and others, *Data Processing in 1980-85,* John Wiley, New York.
35. von Neumann, John, *The General and Logical Theory of Automata.*
36. Levy, David, *Computers are now Chess Masters,* New Scientists, (London), July 1978.
37. Kay and Goldberg, *Personal Dynamic Media,* Computer, March, 1977.

Glossary

Access time   time taken to complete delivery of information from storage or to complete storage where it is required.

Accumulator   part of the logical-arithmetic unit of a computer, which can be used for such intermediate operations as storage to form algebraic sums.

Active storage   memory which requires power to retain its contents, or part of control logic which holds information as it is turned into motion.

Address space   the number of separate locations provided or occupied by a device.

Algorithm   a rule or procedure for solving a mathematical problem usually arising from a repetitive or sequential operation.

Analogue (*or* linear)   a system where the output signal bears a continuous relationship to the input signal, as opposed to the discontinuous relationship exhibited by digital systems.

Architecture   operating characteristics of a control system, control unit or computer.

Automation	the technique of making a process or system automatic.
Bandwidth	the frequency range of a system: e.g. a voice channel needs a lower bandwidth than the image transmission of a T.V.
Batch processing	a type of computer operation in which each program is completed before the next is started.
Binary	a digital system where only two levels of signal are used, such as on/off, high/low or 0/1.
Bipolar	semiconductor devices where the gain is obtained by interaction of positive and negative charge carriers.
Bit	basically, one of the two values of a binary digit (0 and 1).
Bubble memory	data storage in magnetic spots that look like bubbles floating on a semiconductor chip.
Bus	a conductor used for transmitting signals between elements.
Byte	an eight bit binary number: i.e. a code with a range of 28 symbols.
Carterphone decision	a US Supreme Court decision that permitted the connection of any approved equipment made by any manufacturer (i.e., not just AT&T) to the telephone network.
CCD (Charge-coupled-device)	storage device in which information is stored in packets of minute electrical charges, and used as the basis for switching circuits.

Central processing unit (CPU)	the arithmetic, control units and working memory of a computer system (see Microprocessor).
Chips (*or* **die**)	small piece of silicon, which contains one or more circuits, packaged as a unit.
CNC	a numerical control (see N.C.) in which a dedicated, stored program computer performs some or all of the basic numerical control functions.
Coaxial	usually refers to parallel cabling on the same axis.
Compiler	a program which translates high-level computer languages into machine code (see machine code).
Computer	a sequential clock device capable of accepting information in the form of signals or symbols, which performs prescribed operations on the information and which delivers the results via an output device.
Digital	a system that handles information as numbers; or the representation of data in discrete or numerical form.
Digital computer	a computer that operates on symbolic data, by performing arithmetic and logic operations.
Discrete device	a single function, packaged, component, such as a transistor or a diode.
Distributed data processing	an arrangement whereby several intelligent terminals perform, on-site, tasks on their own and only refer to the mainframe when additional computing power is needed or for information combination by the mainframe.

Downtime	the period when a device or system is inoperative.
Electron beam machining	the use of a focussed electron beam to trace a pattern on a material.
Facsimile	method of reproducing an original document at a remote location by electronic communications: usually over telephone networks but also transmitted by satellite or radio communications.
Feedback	the control of a machine or system on the basis of its *actual* performance rather than its *expected* performance.
Flip flop	a device capable of assuming two stable states (such as a two position switch).
Floppy discs	flexible discs used for mass storage in computer systems.
FORTRAN	a high-level computer language designed to solve arithmetic and logical programs.
Front end	the input part of a system.
High-level language	a language allowing the programmer to write programs in statements or commands which resemble 'English'.
Integrated circuit (IC)	a semiconductor device where interconnected active and passive circuit elements are manufactured in a single piece of material (usually silicon) and which forms a functional electronic circuit of transistors, resistors, diodes etc.
Intelligent terminals	a computer peripheral that contains logic and memory enabling it to carry out some processing tasks without reference to the mainframe.

Interface	either an imaginary line drawn to point out differences between portions of a system, or a program or circuit designed to handle discontinuities in a system.
Josephson function	a superconducting semiconductor device operated at cryogenic (near absolute zero) temperatures.
LCD display	liquid crystal display
LED display	light-emitting diode display
Logic gate	circuit function which controls the flow of information, providing an output signal only when the input signals are in prescribed states.
LSI (large-scale-integration)	integrated circuits containing from 100-5,000 logic gates or 1,000-16,000 memory bits.
Linkage	a means of linking information between different routines.
Machine code (*or* language)	a step-by-step language written in a series of bits understandable by a computer CPU. This 'first level' language compares to 'second level' assembly language or a 'third level' compiler language.
Mainframe	a medium/large computer without peripherals.
Mask	a photographic plate with the integrated circuit pattern needed for wafer fabrication.
Memory	store for digital information, in a form that can be understood by a computer. In semiconductor memories data may be stored in the form of electrical charges, as voltage, current levels or gas bubbles.

Microcomputer	a single silicon chip containing a microprocessor as well as memory: in future, probably, some input/output facilities too.
Microelectronics	the technology and manufacture of miniature electronic components or functional circuits.
Microprocessor (MPU)	the central processing unit of a computer contained in an LSI circuit, in one or more chips.
Minicomputer	originally a computer much smaller in size, capacity and software than larger mainframe computers. However, the development of microcircuit-based computers is blurring the distinction between micro, mini and mainframe, and between mainframe and peripherals or terminals.
MOS (Metal-oxide-silicon)	a very low power transistor device controlled by voltage rather than current.
MSI (Medium-scale-integration)	integrated circuits containing from 12-100 logic gates or 100-1,000 memory bits.
Multiplexing	the use of a single device for many purposes; usually refers to communications channels.
Nanosecond	one thousandth of a microsecond (i.e. one thousandth of a millionth of a second).
Numerical control (NC)	control system in which motion develops in response to numerically coded commands.
PABX	private automatic branch telephone exchange.
Peripheral	any auxiliary and storage devices — such as high-speed printers or magnetic discs —

Glossary

	which may be placed under the control of the central computer.
Photolithography	an optical mask or direct copying method of achieving a two dimensional pattern on a suitable surface.
Plug compatible	usually refers to any computer made by an independent manufacturer to run on the software of one of the large mainframe manufacturers, such as IBM or Burroughs.
Programming language	a set of instructions understood by a computer system.
RAM (Random access memory)	a memory in which information can be handled from any storage position.
Ring main	a system where a power supply wire is connected at both ends to the power supply.
ROM (Read-only-memory)	a memory which contains permanent data that can be read but not altered.
Semiconductor	any material that acts as a conductor of electrical current when the voltage acting on it is above a certain level and as a resistor when the voltage is below a certain level. Silicon is the most widely used such material in microelectronics.
Software	programs, routines and documents associated with a computer.
Solid state physics	the study of materials in their solid form.
Transistor	an active semiconductor device used as a switch or an amplifier.
Uptime	the time during which a machine or system is operating.

Viewdata	a system which enables a T.V. user to communicate with a computer system via a telephone line and have information projected on his/her screen.
VLSI (Very-large-scale-integration)	integrated circuit containing at least 5,000 logic gates or more than 16,000 memory bits i.e. 16k and 64k RAM memory chips.
Wafer	a slice of semiconductor material (usually silicon) used in manufacture of integrated circuits.
Word	a basic unit in a computer memory. For most microprocessors, for instance, this consists of 4, 8, 12 or 16 bits. An n-bit word can represent 2^n possible operations.
Yield	the ratio of acceptable to the total number of semi-conductor devices off the production line.

Bibliography and references

General bibliography

Iann Barron and Ray Curnow, *The Future with Microelectronics,* Frances Pinter.
Ernest Braun and Stuart MacDonald, *Revolution in Miniature,* Cambridge University Press.
James Martin, *Telecommunications and the Computer,* Prentice-Hall.
James Martin, *Future Developments in Telecommunications,* Prentice-Hall.
Norbert Wiener, *The Human use of Human Beings,* Doubleday.

Reports and studies

L'Informatisation de la Societe, Documentation Francaises, 1978.
The Strategic Impact of Intelligent Electronics in the United States and Western Europe, 1977-1978, Arthur D. Little Ltd, 1979.
The Microcomputers Marketplace in Western Europe, 1978-86, Pactel, 1979.

The Business Communications Marketplace in Western Europe, 1978-86, Pactel, 1978.
The Microprocessor Industry, Creative Strategies International, 1979.

References

Blackhurst, Tumlir and Marian, *Trade Liberalisation, Protectionism and Interdependence*, (The GATT, Geneva, 1977).
de Bono, Edward, *Opportunities*, Associated Business Programmes, 1978.
Bell, Daniel, *The Cultural Contradictions of Capitalism*, Basic Books, New York.
Shay, Paul, *The Consumer Revolution is Coming*, Marketing, September, 1978.
Barron and Curnow, *The Future with Microelectronics*, Frances Pinter.
Technology and the American Economy, Report of the National Commission on Technology, Automation and Economic Progress, US Government Printing Office, February 1966.
Anderla, Georges, *Information in 1985, A Forecasting Study of Information Needs and Resources*, OECD, Paris, 1973.
Hines, Colin, *The Chips are Down*, Earth Resources, London.
Bell, Daniel, *The Coming of Postindustrial Society*, Basic Books, New York.
Gershuny, I.I., *After Industrial Society?* Macmillan, 1978.
Anderla, Georges, *Information in 1985*, OECD, Paris, 1973.
Boulding, Kenneth, *The Diminishing Returns of Science*, New Scientist, London, March 25, 1971.
Bezier, P.E., *Numerical Control: Mathematics and Applications*, John Wiley, New York.
Understanding Solid State Electronics, Texas Instruments Learning Center.
Hamilton and Howard, *Basic Circuit Engineering*, McGraw-Hill, 1975.

Weiner, Charles, *How the Transistor Emerged*, IEEE Spectrum, January, 1973.
Proceedings of the Symposium of the IRE-AIEE-RTMA, Washington, D.C., May 1952.
Petritz, Richard, L., *Contributions to Materials Technology to Semiconductor Devices*, Proceedings of IRE, 1962.
Barker, H.A., *The Microprocessor in Control*, The Institution of Electrical Engineers, October, 1978.
Noyce, Robert, *Microelectronics*, Scientific American, September, 1977.
Barron & Curnow, *The Future with Microelectronics*, Frances Pinter, 1979.
The Strategic Impact of Intelligent Electronics in the United States and Western Europe, 1977-1987, Arthur D. Little Ltd.
Orme, M., *Shopfloor Computers*, Engineering Today, February, 1978.
L'Informatisation de la Societe, Documentation Francaises, 1978.
The Microcomputers Marketplace in Western Europe, 1978-86, Pactel.
Barker, H.A., *The Microprocessor in Control*, IEE.
Hilburn and Julich, *Microcomputers/Microprocessors: Hardware, Software and Applications*, Prentice-Hall Inc.
Roberts, Derek, *Chips-Challenges and Opportunities*, New Scientist, (London) June 8, 1978.
Braun and MacDonald, *Revolution in Miniature*, Cambridge University Press.
Orme, M., *Inmos-Mixing Memory and Desire*, Datalink, November, 1978.
Curnow and Freeman, *Product and Process Change Arising from the Microprocessor Revolution and Some Economic and Social Issues*, Sussex University, Science Policy Research Unit, 1978.
McWhorter, Eugene, W., *The Small Electronic Calculator*, Scientific American, March 1976.
Macintosh, I.M., *Dominant Trends Affecting the Future of the Semiconductor Industry*, Radio and Electronic Engineer, February, 1973.

Dolotta, Bernstein et al, *Data Processing in 1980-85,* John Wiley, New York.

von Neumann, John, *The General and Logical Theory of Automata.*

Levy, David, *Computers are now Chess Masters,* New Scientist (London), July 1978.

Kay and Goldberg, *Personal Dynamic Media,* Computer, March, 1977.

Index

AT&T 34, 113, 126, 170, 177-9, 183-6
Advancement engineering 9
Amdahl, Gene 56, 86
   470 computer 86
Anderla, Georges 49-50
Apple II 152
Applications, potential 75, 77-80, 147-72
Assembly lines 26-8, 34
Automatic controls, history 58-9
Automation of production 34-5, 88
Automobiles, accessories 22-3
   industry 28, 34, 73, 76, 111, 161-7
   learning curve, 166-7
   main areas of electronics research 163
   potential microprocessor applications 77, 161-7

Babbage, Charles 59
Barron, Iann 28, 52, 138, 140, 143, 147, 178, 181
Bell, David 41
Bell Laboratories 61, 91, 184
Blackhurst, Richard 2
Bohr, Nils, xii, 75
Boulding, Kenneth 50
Bowmar 150

Brindley, James 58-9
Bundling 87
Business structures 41-4, 101-4, 122-3, 143-5
   infrastructures 113-4, 184-5

CSERB 28, 52, 140-1, 178, 181
Calculators
   history 66-7
   SR-59 109
   see also Pocket calculators
Capital costs 111-2
Cars *see* Automobiles
Cash registers, 7, 12, 34, 99
Check-out terminals 26
Children 109
China, microelectronics industry 15-6, 25
Chips *see* Silicon chips
Circuits, complexity levels 13
   numbers of components, — 1960-80, 65
   see also Memory circuits, VLSI circuits
Commodore Co 150
Communications networks 173-90
Communications satellites 178, 185-6, 189-90
Communications terminals 89, 157-8, 169-72, 179-80

Computer
  effects of microprocessors on 87-97
  generations 95-5
  industry, Japan 7-8
    USA see under names of firms, e.g. IBM
    USSR 14-5
  plug-compatibles 86
  principles of 68-9
  software 85-6, 93, 97, 106, 109, 115-9, 143-4, 152-4
  see also Programming; Solid state software
Computer-aided design 89
  instruction 95-6
Computer-augmented conferences 43
Computer-information revolution 12, 37, 41, 173-4
Computer networks 173-90
Computer simulations 38-9, 93-4
Computer see also Home Computers; Ultra-intelligent machines
Computers, Systems and Electronics Requirements Board 28, 52, 140-141, 178, 181
Confederations of entrepreneurs 42
Confravision 43-4
Consultants 106-7
Consumers, behaviour 71-2, 95, 148
  in Western countries 17-23, 25
  in Japan 23-5
  categories 19-20
Control systems 101-2, 107
Corporate structures 41-4, 101-4, 122-3, 143-5
  infrastructures 113-4, 184-5
Corrigan, Wilfred 132
Cray 1 121
Creative Strategies International 154
Crook, Colin 132
Cross-file computer systems 102
Curnow, Ray 28, 52, 181

Databases 83, 84, 86, 88-9, 96, 100, 102, 112
Data transmission 46, 88, 96
  see also Telematics
de Bono, Edward 8
de Butts, John 184
Defence industries, potention microprocessor applications 79
Delphi methods xv, 33, 76
Demand patterns 181
Dertouzos, Michael 160
Design 70-1
  problems 71, 104-6
Design engineers 71-2, 100, 104-6, 112
  designer interaction 136-7
  training of 106
Development systems 107
Dick, A.B. 182
Diebold, John 84
Diffusion rate 31-2
Digital computers, history 59-60
Digital watches 21, 34, 72, 99, 158
  effects on clock and watch industries 99-100
Dijiskra, Edsgar 118
Discretionary incomes 19-20
Distributed DP 83, 85, 96, 159
  advantages 90
  implications for management 100-4, 112
Dummer, G.W.A. 62

EMS 187-8
ENIAC 59, 64
Economics xiv-xv, 1-25, 52-6
  international aspects 16-7
Economic growth, Less Developed Countries 1-2, 12
Electronic calculators see Calculators
Electronic intelligence 27, 33, 82-3
Electronic message systems 187-8
Electronics, Computing, and Information technology, 28-9
Electronics City, Tokyo 23

Electronics industry *see*
   Semiconductor industry
Employment 27-8, 32-7
Engineering continuum 57, 65-6
Europe, electronics industry 131-2
   office equipment industry 182-3
   see also UK, semiconductor
   industry
Exxon, Qyx word processor 113-4
   vs IBM 113-4

Facsimile 182-3, 187
Factory robots *see* Robots
Faggin, Frederico 64
Fairchild 124, 134-6, 141-2, 145
Feedback mechanisms 34
   history 58-9
Ferranti 16, 132
Fiat 34
Forecasting *see* Future
Fujitsu 129-30, 179
Future prospects xii, xiv-xviii, 22-5, 70-80
   applications 75, 77-80
   employment 35-7
   forecasting flaws 75-9
   of silicon products 147-72
   problems 70-2
   social and political environment 29-48
   see also Management;
   Semiconductors; Telematics;
   Ultra-intelligent machines
'Future with microelectronics' 28, 52

GEC 135, 182
GEISCO 180
General Motors 163-6
Gould 135-6

Hammer, Carl 15
Hewlett-Packard 37
High level languages 115-8
History 57-67
   semiconductor industry 124-6
Hixon symposium 192

Hoff, Ted 64
Hogan, Lester 124-5, 138-9, 145
Hollerith, Herman 59
Holography 190
Home computers 20-1, 38, 43-4, 72, 93, 97, 109, 151-9
Home of the future 151-61
Human engineering problems xii, 98-119

IBM 7, 13, 46, 56, 59, 86-8, 125-6 138, 143, 145, 177, 179, 183-6
   360: 85, 101
   1401: 85, 101
   4300: 87
   Selectric 113-4
   systems network architecture 180-182
   vs. Exxon 113-4
'Industrial arthritis' 2-5
Industrial control,
   potential microprocessor
   applications 78-9
Industry *see* Semiconductor
   industry
Information 45-6
   explosion 49-50
   for management 101-2
   for industry 173-4
   production factor 39-41, 88-9
   see also Databases
Information-processing pathologies 83-4, 93
'Informatisation de la Societe'
   (Nora report) 6, 28, 36, 45, 81
Inmos 137-45
Inner-directed consumer group 20-1
Instrumentation, potentials of
   microprocessors in 78
Integrated circuits *see* Silicon chips
Intel Corp 63-5, 86, 107, 124, 128, 141, 143, 145, 152
   8086: 116, 119
Intelligent terminals *see* Communications terminals

International Data Corporation 174, 181
Iso 46
Japan
  economy 4-5
  electronics industry 7-13, 98-9, 129-31, 178-9
  Ministry of International Trade and Industry 6, 11, 179
  robot programme 34
  technology policy 6-11, 24-5
Jigs 58
'Job-killers' 27-29
  see also Unemployment

Kearney survey 84
Keynesian economics 53-5
Kilby, Jack 62
Kondratief cycles 53
Korea, electronics industry 132-3
Kuhn, Thomas 143
Kvamme, Floyd 68, 72

LSI circuits see Silicon chips
Languages, programming 108-10, 115-9
Learning curve, impact on pricing and production 22, 123, 127-30, 150-1, 166-7
Libraries 50, 190
Licensing 42
Lindbeck, Assar 3
List, Bernard H. 96
Little, Arthur D. 36-7, 84, 88, 101, 156, 182
Lock-in 83, 85-6, 107, 117
Logic-gates 91
Losty, Havard 135

MITI see Japan, Ministry of International Trade and Industry
MITS 21, 93, 151-2
MPU (Intel) 64
McGill, Archie 181
Machine codes 115-7
Macintosh, Ian 136-7

Mackintosh Consultants 145, 156, 158
Madland, Glen 133
Management problems xii, 98-119
  infrastructural problems 113-4
  main lessons for management 102-3
Management services 101-2
Marketing 148-9, 151-4, 184
Marriott, David 135
Marxist economics 55
Materials science 63
Materials science 63
Mechanical engineering industry 29, 34
Medical diagnosis 27
Memory circuits 70, 116, 140
Microcomputers 149-59
  programming 13
  see also Home computers; Pocket calculators
Microprocessors
  definition 68
  engineering 69-70
  history 63-7
  potential applications 75, 77-9, 147-72
  primary roles 108
  programming see Programming, microcomputers
  scope and prospects 68-80
Military expenditures 13-4
Miniaturisation, history of 60-2
Minuteman project 62
Moore, Gordon 124, 128, 141
Mostek 133, 138-9, 150
Motorola 124-5
  MC 68000: 116

National Cash Register 34
National Enterprise Board 137
National Semiconductor 142-4
Networks see Distributed DP; Telematics
Nora, Simon 6, 28, 36, 45, 81

Noyce, Robert 63-4, 67, 73-4, 120, 124, 131, 141, 143

OECD studies 33, 50-1
OPEC 176
Office employment 32
Office equipment 78, 131-3
Offices of the future 181-3
Oil, competition between telematic & oil companies 175-6
world reserves 176
Opportunity-seeking 8-9
Optical fibres 179

Pactel 182-3
Paperless office 32
Pascal, Blaise 59
Peripherals 110
see also specific items of equipment e.g. Word processors
Personal computers see Home computers
Petritz, Richard 137, 140-1, 143, 145
Philippines, computer industry 16-7
Plug-compatibles 86
Pocket calculators xiv-xv, 21, 71-2, 81, 121
history 150-1
Political environment 26-56
Political problems 44-5
Portability 117
Post-industrial society 17, 24, 41-5
definition 41-2
Presidential Commission on Technology 31
Prices 22, 122-3, 127-8, 145, 150-1
Product design see Design
Product planning 102-3
Programmers 100, 104, 108-10
Programming
languages 108-10, 115-9
microcomputers 13, 100, 106-10, 115-9, 143-4

problems 71, 84-5, 93, 96, 107-9
see also Computers, software; Solid state software
Prospects see Future prospects

RAM 70, 116, 140
RCA 76
Radio Shack TRS 80: 152
Registers 116
Reliability 10, 61-2, 110-1
Research 125-7
Robots 26-8, 34
Rockwell 109
Royal Radar Establishment 62
Russia see USSR
Ryad computers 14

SBS 117, 180-1
SIC see Silicon chips
Sagan, Carl 193
Sales 73, 134
Satellites 178, 185-6, 189-90
Savings, consumer behaviour 18-9
Schlumberger 136
Schroeder, Paul 138-9
Second industrial revolution 12, 37, 41, 173-4
Semiconductor industry 120-46
force-feeding the market 120-1
history 124-6
main characteristics 122-3
making the products usable 121-2
prices 122-3, 127-8
Semiconductors
flow through industry 105
main qualities xii-xiii
see also under specific headings, e.g. Silicon chips
Sevin, M.J. 138-9
Shockley, William 124-5
Siemens 27-8, 32
Signal processing 91
Silicon-based integrated circuits see Silicon chips
Silicon chips xiii, 62-8, 70, 83, 86, 91, 140-2, 145

advantages of 77
costs 74-5
see also Memory circuits;
   Semiconductor industry;
   VLSI circuits
Silicon products 147-72
   general characteristics 147-50
   see also under names of specific
      products, e.g. Personal
      calculators
Silicon Valley 124-5
Sinclair Radionics 10
Social environment 26-56
Software *see* Computer software;
   Programming
Solid state software 109, 154
Steel industry 2
'Strategic impact of intelligent
   electronics in the US and Western
   Europe, 1977-87' 36-7
Subcontracting 42
Systems approach *see* Distributed
   DP; Telematics
Systems houses 106-7
Szuprowics, Bohdan 14

TASI 91-2, 112
Taxes 18
Technology policy, Japan 6-11, 24
Technology transfer 1, 16-7, 24-5
Telecommunications, potential
   microprocessor applications 78
Telematics 46, 50, 90-3, 173-90
   areas affected by 92-3
   competition between telematic
      and oil companies 175-6
   economic aspects 177
Telenet 175
Telephone industry 34, 37, 111-2,
   177-8, 183
Telephone services 157-8, 160, 169-71
Teletext 187
Television receiver developments
   171-2

Terminals 89, 157-8, 169-72, 179-80
Texas Instruments 10, 62, 93, 109,
   125-8, 140, 150-4, 160
Think tanks xv
Time-assignment-speech-
   interpolation 91-2, 112
'Tomorrow in Electronics' 145
Transistors, history 61, 63
Tumlir, Jan 2

UIM 191-6
UK
   Post Office 178
   semiconductor industry 137-43
USA
   automobile industry 73, 76
   Department of Commerce 30
USSR, microelectronics industry 13-5, 25
Ultra-intelligent machines 191-6
Unemployment 27-8, 32-7
Universal Data Machines 150

Veblen, Thorstein 55-6
VLSI circuits 81, 86, 87, 112, 121,
   126, 129, 140-1, 144
Video recorders 12
Viewdata 112, 187
Voice synthesisers 160-1
Volkswagen 28, 34
von Neumann, John 59, 61, 192

Wasserman, Jerry 98
Weizenbaum, Joe 118
Westcott, John 156
Western Electric 34
Whitney, Eli 58
Wiener, Norbert 36, 57, 59-60
Word processing 26, 89, 181
Workforce, Japanese 8
World economy 1-25

'zero-sum' game 40, 139
Zilog 116, 119, 128, 139, 145

LIBRARY OF DAVIDSON COLLEGE